CURRENT AFRICAN ISSUES 40

I0025477

The African economy and its role in the world economy

Arne Bigsten and Dick Durevall

NORDISKA AFRIKAINSTITUTET, UPPSALA 2008

A background paper commissioned by the Nordic Africa Institute
for the Swedish Government White Paper on Africa.

INDEXING TERMS:
Economic performance
International economic relations
International trade
Capital movements
Globalization
Structural adjustment
Economic and social development
Policy making
Africa south of Sahara
Sweden

The opinions expressed in this volume are those of the authors
and do not necessarily reflect the views of the Nordic Africa Institute.

Language checking: Peter Colenbrander
ISSN 0280-2171
ISBN 978-91-7106-625-1 (print)
ISBN 978-91-7106-631-2 (electronic)
© The authors and Nordiska Afrikainstitutet 2008
Printed in Sweden by Elanders Sverige AB, Mölnlycke 2008
Grafisk form Today Press AB

CONTENTS

List of Tables

List of Figures

Acronyms

ACP	Group of 77 countries from the African, Caribbean and Pacific Regions
AERC	African Economic Research Consortium
AfDF	African Development Fund
AGOA	African Growth and Opportunity Act
CAP	Common Agricultural Policy
DFID	Department for International Development (UK)
EC	European Commission
EFTA	Economic Free Trade Area
EPA	Economic Partnership Agreement
EU	European Union
EU25	European Union with all 25 members
FDI	Foreign Direct Investment
GDF	Global Development Finance
GDP	Gross Domestic Product
GNI	Gross National Income
GSP	Generalised System of Pretences
G8	Group of Eight
HIPC	Highly Indebted Poor Country
IDA	International Development Association
IMF	International Monetary Fund
LDC	Least Developed Country
MDG	Millennium Development Goals
MDG1	Millennium Development Goal 1 (halving poverty by 2015)
MDRI	Multilateral Debt Relief Initiative
NTB	Non-Tariff Barrier
OECD	Organisation of Economic Cooperation and Development
PPP	Purchasing Power Parity
UNAIDS	United Nations and the Joint United Nations Programme on HIV/AIDS
UNDP	United Nations Development Programme
WDI	World Development Indicators
WTO	World Trade Organisation

Executive Summary

After a period of falling per capita incomes that started in the 1970s, Africa finally saw a turn-around from about 1995, with initially modest increases in per capita incomes. However, the last few years have actually seen average per capita incomes in Africa grow by above 3% on average, partly due to the resource boom, but also due to improved economic policies.

Sub-Saharan Africa is a very small player in the global economy. At current exchange rates, sub-Saharan Africa produced only 1.4% of global GDP in 2005 and had an average per capita income that was 1/41 of that of the high income countries. Adjusting for differences in purchasing power, the gap shrinks to 1/16, which is still enormous. In PPP terms, Africa is clearly the poorest region in the world.

The growth experiences vary considerably across countries and over time. The countries that receive much Swedish aid today generally did badly in the 1980s, somewhat better in the 1990s and many have been doing very well since the turn of the century. The average for the main recipients of Swedish aid in 2001–05 is 2.2% growth in per capita income per year, which is slightly better than the sub-Saharan African average of 2.0%. Civil war has been an important cause of bad economic performance in several countries in Africa, and the elimination of remaining conflicts as well as the maintenance of peace is very important for progress in poverty reduction.

The industrial sector, including manufacturing, has not been able to expand as hoped for at independence or as it has done in Asia. The import-substitution policy that was pursued to support manufacturing growth in Africa achieved some results in the 1960s, but the policies did not lead to the creation of a manufacturing sector that could compete internationally. In 1960, sub-Saharan Africa supplied 4.2% of world exports, but by the turn of the century this had shrunk to only 1.4%. By 2005, however, Africa had increased its global market share some-what due to the boom in natural resources such as oil, and this is, of course, also one of the reasons for the growth acceleration. The bulk of African exports are raw materials, agricultural products and also tourism services. There is still no breakthrough in terms of manufacturing exports. Even if Africa is of marginal importance in world trade, African economies are more dependent on the world market than are those of high income countries.

Africa is not only the poorest region in the world, but it also has an increasing share of the world's population. The population growth rate is declining in Africa as in other regions, but since the region is lagging economically, it has not come as far as the other regions in the demographic transition process. The result of this is that the sub-Saharan African share of the world population has increased from 7.4% to 11.5% over a 45 year period.

Economic growth requires investments, and investments are financed by savings. They can be domestic savings or international savings transferred to the country. The African region saved 17.6% of GDP in 2005, which is low compared to the fast growers in Asia. Official financial flows or aid were US$ 30.5 bn in 2005, foreign direct investments US$ 16.6 bn and other private transfers, which include various forms of private remittances, were US$ 9.8 bn. Foreign direct investments in particular have increased in recent years, mainly in the natural resource sector.

Still, the flow of aid to Africa can be seen as a response to the small volume of private capital flows and, of course, it is also a response to the state of poverty in the region. Africa receives more aid per capita than any other major region. There are a few countries with extremely high aid dependency ratios, mainly those countries that have emerged from civil war and internal conflict and are in a rebuilding phase. Other countries have high ratios because of debt write-offs, while others have gradually done better economically and have become 'donor-darlings'.

Has aid to Africa been effective in terms of its impact on economic growth? The most recent studies find that there is a significantly positive effect of aid on growth, although they are less positive in the tropics (and many African countries fall into this category). This result is not generally conditional on good policies, although good policies of course make outcomes better.

Private remittances to Africa have shown an increasing trend, according to official statistics, and the official flows are estimated to be about 2.5% of GDP, which is considerably less than flows to other developing countries. One important positive feature of remittance incomes is that the flow has been rather stable, while both aid and FDI have fluctuated considerably. Remittance incomes provide an opportunity for low-income households to access formal financial services.

At the Millennium Summit of 2000, world leaders agreed on a set of common development targets, the Millennium Development Goals, for development efforts until 2015. In 2005, proposals for massive increases in aid to Africa in particular were presented by the UN and the Commission for Africa. In terms of the promises made by the Western countries, for example at the G8 meeting at Gleneagles in 2005, the aid flow to Africa should increase rapidly during the next few years. There is also agreement within the EU that all (the old) members will give at least 0.56% of GNI as aid by 2010 and 0.7% by 2015. Sweden already surpasses this figure, while the average for the whole of (old) EU was 0.35% in 2004. Whether the member countries will live up to these promises remains to be seen.

One of the most notable aspects of the current process of globalisation is the increase in trade between sub-Saharan Africa and Asia, particularly China and India. African exports to Asia grew by over 10% per year from the early 1990s to 2003. In parallel with increasing trade, Chinese FDIs have risen rapidly but from a low level. Chinese companies have invested in various sectors, including oil, mining, fishing, telecommunications, construction and power generation. Moreover, Chinese companies have been setting up plants to circumvent quota regimes in the West for textiles and clothing.

The increase in trade with China and India implies both threats and opportunities. First, the effects of a natural resource boom are difficult to handle for countries with weak institutions, and there is a risk of domestic conflict, or at least gross misallocation of government income resources. Second, imports of cheap manufactured goods are a threat to Africa's manufacturing sector and might lead to de-industrialisation. There are also threats related to FDI. Chinese firms tend to invest in extractive industries with few links to local firms. They also use their own labour to a high degree and do not invest much in African workers.

On the other hand, China's trade and investment in sub-Saharan Africa is an opportunity for economic growth and integration into the world economy. Growth rates are higher than for decades, which no doubt is related to the commodity boom induced by China and India. Moreover, the increase in trade has made cheap consumer goods available to many Africans, thus raising living standards. And investments in production and infrastructure are bound to have many beneficial effects. Furthermore, China and India have huge and expanding consumer markets.

The final impact of the Asian drivers is determined by policies adopted primarily in sub-Saharan Africa, but also by China and India. Donors and international organisations also have an important role to play, providing technical assistance to strengthen trade-related institutions and improve policy implementation.

The success of debt reduction efforts depends on the ability of debtor countries to achieve high growth and foreign exchange earnings. This did not happen in sub-Saharan Africa in the 1980s and 1990s: so many countries were left with huge official debts after two decades of structural adjustment lending. Most highly indebted countries were therefore in Africa. The HIPC programme was initiated by the World Bank and the IMF in 1996 and an extended version of it was launched in 1999. The purpose was to reduce the debts of highly indebted countries to sustainable levels, that is a level at which they could service their debts.

The HIPC programme led to some debt reduction, but many countries were left with debts they were still unable to serve. The G8 proposal from June 2005, now called the Multi-lateral Debt Relief Initiative (MDRI), therefore set out to cancel 100% of the debt that heavily indebted poor countries owed to the African Development fund (AfDF), International Development Association and the International Monetary Fund. Complete debt reduction occurs when these LDCs have reached the completion point under the HIPC arrangement. This initiative is expected to result in a further reduction of debts by about US $50 bn. The cancellation is contingent on sound macroeconomic performance, implementation of a Poverty Reduction Strategy and public expenditure management systems.

Debt relief has two major impacts. First, it influences the incentives for private investment. Second, it has a fiscal effect. The latter makes it possible to increase poverty-related expenditures. For the 29 countries that had benefited from debt relief by 2005, poverty related expenditures have increased from about 6% of GDP in 1999 to about 9% in 2005. This is a significant improvement, but it should be noted that although extensive debt reductions in African countries have taken place, the reduction in actual debt service has been rather limited. Many countries did not service their debt properly. The total sub-Saharan Africa debt stock ceased to increase in the mid-1990s and there has been a clear decline in total outstanding debt in the last few years. Actual debt service has declined, and this has increased the room for domestic expenditures.

It is not easy to measure how the debt reductions have affected African growth rates, but it seems reasonable to assume that it has had some positive impact on investment incentives. It should have relieved the pressure of taxation (current and future) on investors and the general public. It has also increased the scope in budgets for both poverty-oriented expenditures and growth-enhancing expenditures. There may be negative incentive effects, though.

About 25 million people in sub-Saharan Africa are infected with HIV, and approximately 2.8 million became infected in 2006. Hence, in most parts the HIV/AIDS epidemic is not only a health problem but a human disaster with far-ranging social and economic consequences.

Many studies address the links between HIV/AIDS and economic growth. Nonetheless, there is still not a consensus on how the epidemic affects income per capita. However, most recent studies obtain large negative effects. One study finds that the rate of per capita output will be between 0.3 and 0.7 percentage points lower than without HIV/AIDS over the period 2000–10, and another that HIV/AIDS has reduced Africa's per capita growth rate by 0.7

percentage points. Yet another study reports that the average marginal impact on per capita income growth of a 1% increase in HIV prevalence rate in sub-Saharan Africa is -0.59%.

A more surprising result is found in studies by Alvin Young, who argues that the epidemic will increase economic growth in countries seriously affected by HIV/AIDS. The argument is that HIV/AIDS reduces fertility, and its decline outweighs the negative effects of the decrease in human capital. The important role of fertility is due to its impact on the ratio between the number of children and elderly, and the number of adults of working age (the dependency ratio). A favourable development in the dependency ratio has a strong impact on per capita GDP growth.

Recent studies have contradicted Young. They argue that HIV/AIDS's main impact is through its effect on adult mortality. An increase in adult mortality makes people more myopic and thus reduces investment in both physical capital and education. In addition, it leads to higher fertility: families have more children when the uncertainty of survival of their offspring into adulthood is high. Hence AIDS, by increasing adult mortality, has a strong negative impact on growth in per capita income. Some recent studies provide empirical evidence in favour of the hypothesis.

An argument against macroeconomic studies of HIV/AIDS is the difficulty of capturing all important mechanisms in an economic model and evaluating their relative impacts. Moreover, there might be nonlinear relationships. There is no reason to believe that the effect of the disease increases in line with prevalence when it rises from 1% to 20%. Hence, the epidemic can cause sudden large changes that have not been observed yet. One example discussed in the literature is the collapse of institutions such as the judiciary, the policy force and other government bodies. Such a scenario would imply a sharp increase in poverty.

Most research shows that HIV/AIDS increases poverty and worsens income distribution. For instance, simulations of the impact of HIV/AIDS on poverty over a ten year period in four sub-Saharan countries show that even in cases where HIV/AIDS does not reduce per capita income, poverty increases. The size of the effect depends on how many people live near the poverty line and the prevalence rates among them. For example, poverty increases by 10 percentage points in Swaziland, 6 percentage points in Kenya and 1.5 percentage points in Ghana. Besides, the income distribution becomes more unequal in all countries.

The epidemic is also likely to have a negative influence on human capital and human knowledge in general. First, there is the direct effect when experienced or educated workers become ill or die. Second, both the quantity and quality of schooling are likely to decrease. Third, there is less parent-to-child transfer of knowledge.

A recent study that evaluated the impact of HIV/AIDS on education in seven sub-Saharan African countries found that children living in areas with HIV prevalence rates of 10% complete about 0.5 fewer years of schooling than children living in areas without HIV. Another study, using data on initially non-orphaned Tanzanian children in 1991–94, evaluated the impact of orphanhood on educational attainment in 2004. It found that maternal orphans permanently lose on average one year of schooling. Both these studies indicate that the impact of HIV/AIDS on the level of education is substantial: the mean years of schooling among adults in is about 4.7 years.

There is strong gender aspect of HIV/AIDS. Women constitute the majority of those who are HIV-positive (57% in sub-Saharan Africa), and the prevalence rates among those aged 15–24 are many times higher for females than for males. Women also carry a large part of the burden of HIV/AIDS. They take responsibility for the care of those who are ill, on top of a heavy workload. Moreover, when the husband dies, they might lose their assets, including land. And those households that continue farming usually have much lower per capita incomes than when the husbands were alive.

During the last couple of years, the distribution of anti-retroviral therapy to prevent the development of AIDS has expanded significantly in several countries. The availability of treatment is likely to have economic consequences, but so far there are few studies documenting the impact. Nevertheless, initial findings point towards very positive effects on both household incomes and the nutritional status of the children.

In sub-Saharan Africa, women are disadvantaged in many respects, and the situation is worse than in most other parts of the world. According to UNDP's gender-related development index, the best sub-Saharan country is South Africa, which is ranked 120 out of 177 countries, Gabon 123, while almost all the positions from 141 to 177 are occupied by sub-Saharan countries.

Reducing gender inequality is a development goal in its own right, but economic research has mostly focused on its role in promoting economic development. Most research has been at the household level, and there is ample microeconomic evidence that gender relations matter for economic development. Research on the macroeconomic consequences of gender inequality in general is sparse. One reason is the problem of measuring gender inequality. Moreover, the most commonly used measure of inequality, income, is only available for households. The alternative is to use non-income inequality measures of well-being. Hence, macro studies have primarily focused on education, but there are some that use health indicators and social capital, such as women's political participation. Several recent studies find a strong gender effect on economic growth. Gender inequality has a strong impact on economic growth, particularly in sub-Saharan Africa. It is found to explain as much as 30% of the difference in growth rates between Botswana, with high growth and low educational gaps, and Ghana and Niger, with substantial gender inequalities.

Hence, investment in female education appears to have a high pay-off both in terms of economic growth, as well as in reduced gender inequality. And the pay-off is likely to be especially high in sub-Saharan Africa, possibly due to the large imbalances. The results from macroeconomic studies on other aspects of gender inequality, such as health and social capital, are not as strong but point in the same direction.

There has been a brain drain from sub-Saharan Africa for a long time, and it has increased significantly since the 1970s, both in absolute and relative terms. During 1990, for which there is reliable data, 11.7% of the skilled workers worked outside sub-Saharan Africa, and in 2000 the number had increased to 12.9%. The migration of skilled workers varies greatly across regions and countries: in Eastern Africa the migration rate, i.e., the number of skilled workers living outside the region divided by the number of skilled workers in the region, was as high as 18.6% for skilled workers in 2000. And in specific countries the rates were even higher: 42% of those with tertiary education had migrated from Ghana by 2000, 25.6% from Angola and 26.3% from Kenya. The migration rate for Sweden, for example, was 4.4%.

Generally brain drain is considered to be unfavourable for the migrants' home country and favourable to the recipient. However, brain drain does not have only negative effects on those left behind. Migration of skilled workers generates remittances, it improves business and trade networks, increases expected returns to education, and leads to increased knowledge and skills when migrants return home.

Recent studies of the costs and benefits of migration conclude that optimal skilled migration is positive: this means there should be some net skilled migration from poor countries. However, there are distributional consequences: countries with low levels of human capital and large shares of skilled migrants lose. Small countries in sub-Saharan Africa and Central America clearly have too much migration of skilled workers

There is a need for action, both for sub-Saharan countries losing skilled workers and for the recipient countries, as well for donors and international organisations. A recent initiative by DFID in Malawi to top up salaries for health workers and provide incentives to attract Malawian doctors and nurses working abroad to return home, is one interesting attempt to alleviate the problems caused by brain drain.

There is an extensive literature on the trade-growth relationship. This is a somewhat controversial literature since it is hard to show clearly a casual relationship, but it is abundantly clear that the countries that have succeeded in increasing income levels substantially have also been successful in the export markets. There is a range of studies showing that improved access to international markets, for example if EU eliminated various agricultural protection measures, would enhance African incomes significantly. Such reforms would also have a positive distributional impact in the developing countries, since it is farmers and unskilled labour that are most likely to gain from the trade liberalisation.

The aim of the Doha Round was to achieve multilateral, reciprocal, non-discriminatory trade liberalisation. A successful completion of the round would have implied significantly lower levels of protection, although still some way from full free trade. Simulations of the impact show that most of the gains from the likely reforms will end up in the North, while the impact on sub-Saharan Africa specifically would be modest. Thus, the 'concessions' that the EU and other industrialised countries are willing to make would largely benefit themselves. For the Doha Round to really benefit Africa, substantially more is needed. It would be important to transfer some of the gains from the liberalisation from the EU to Africa in the form of more aid, for example, to develop supply capacities in sub-Saharan Africa via improvements in transport and market infrastructure, training and extension.

African countries are at present covered by the EU General System of Preferences, but this does not seem to have had any large effect on African exports. The fact that other parts of the world have done much better in terms of export expansion suggests that African countries suffer from major supply side constraints. In the last couple of years, booming prices for oil and other natural resources has increased export incomes, and sub-Saharan Africa saw incomes from merchandise exports increase by 27% in 2005. Thus, there have been some improvements in recent years because of the resource boom, but how long this will last is an open question.

Sub-Saharan Africa countries not only face tariffs in the developed countries, but also even higher tariffs on their trade with other developing countries. While sub-Saharan African exporters face low barriers in the EU with regard to manufacturing, exports of agricultural goods are more restricted.

EU has a system of trade preferences in place, but it discriminates against LDCs that are not in the ACP group, and they lack reciprocity. EU and the ACP countries did not manage to finalise a new arrangement during the Cotonou trade negotiations, so the WTO granted them an 8-year waiver that expires at the end of 2007. The EPAs, covering trade relations and EU assistance measures plus measures to enhance intra-regional and international integration, therefore need to be put in place shortly (unless another extension can be obtained).

Simulations of the effects of EPAs find that the short-run welfare effects will be limited and that African economies would have relatively more to gain from unilateral liberalisation in relation to all countries, not EU only. Such measures would be more growth enhancing, since they would be less discriminatory. Particularly the LDCs have relatively little to gain with regard to trade from entering into EPAs, since they already have almost free access to the EU market under the 'Everything But Arms' initiative. They will get even better access in the future as the remaining tariffs and quotas on bananas, rice and sugar will be phased out by July 2009. The LDCs will then have full and free market access to the EU market (including the commodities currently subject to the EU's commodity protocols with the ACP countries). However, these countries still face the risk that the EU may use various safeguard clauses to stem export surges and countries may be eliminated from the generous treatment when they graduate from the LDC category. In spite of various problems, the EPA process may have beneficial long-term effects. It needs to be supported by other measures to facilitate export expansion in ACP countries.

For Africa to take off economically, economic agents have to be put in a context where they have incentives and opportunities to invest and to allocate resources efficiently. The economic environment in Africa has not been so benevolent, but it has been improved in many countries in the recent decade. Still, it remains true that the economic environment in Africa is more risky than that in other regions for several reasons. There are, for example, climate risks that make it hard to be a farmer in Africa. There are also economic risks associated with the specialisation of African economies on certain natural resources or crops, for which prices on the world market may fluctuate. There are policy risks in the sense that the political environment is often unstable, and this makes it hard to make long-term investment decisions. In recent years, several political conflicts have escalated into full-blown civil wars, sometimes also drawing in neighbouring countries.

Thus, Africa is a region with unusually high economic risks. This means that investors, domestic as well as international, demand a very high risk premium on their investments in Africa. This holds back African investments. The quality and stability of the economic environment within which economic agents operate depends on the institutional structure, and the quality of the government is, of course, central here. We have argued that the poor quality of institutions and policy is the most important constraint on African growth. There has in recent years been a process of democratisation and some improvement in the functioning of governments, but the low quality of governance is still the most severe development problem in Africa.

The question then is how such incentives for governments can be provided. The normal procedure in a democracy is of course that the government is under the control of the electorate, with the help of the media and various civil society organisations. During the structural adjustment period, democracy in Africa was poor and donors sought to come up with an alternative control mechanism. The poor efficiency of this approach led to increasing scepticism about conditionality, and the debate on ownership followed. This led to reform of the system of conditionalities, with more emphasis on control of policy formulation by the recipient government, but with more extensive exchanges of views with various strata of the society, including donors. This has led to some reduction of policy conditionalities, but is not really a radical departure.

The impact of the predicted increase in aid flows will depend on the modalities for its transfer. A key aim of donors should be to improve governance and implementation capacity in recipient countries. This requires a shift towards governance conditionality combined with technical assistance to build up systems that can handle government resources in a transparent and accountable way.

For this to work, there is need for donor coordination. UNDP has never managed to bring this about although it was its original mandate, while the World Bank and the IMF have had such a role. A possible coordinator in the case of European aid would be the EU, but so far it has not performed this task. Coordination has for many years been very high on the official aid agenda of most donors, but progress has been limited. By shifting towards more general forms of aid such as budget support, donors may reduce the coordination problem and possibly also increase ownership. When different donors finance the same project or programmes, they should appoint one of their number to be the coordinating agent responsible for government contacts and follow up.

The EU and the whole of the OECD have often reiterated the need for policy coherence for development. Sweden has adopted an official policy that seeks to ensure that all policies are consistent with the desire for global development and poverty reduction in poor countries. Policies across various ministries as well as across various countries should thus support the overall goal of development in LDCs and create synergies among themselves. This ambition to achieve policy coherence matters both from the perspective of altruism and of self-interest. The most problematic political areas for policy change of the sort discussed in this paper are not aid policy but trade policy and the CAP. This is a challenge to Swedish and EU policy makers, since changes to the latter areas are probably the most important if we are serious about our commitment to development.

1. Introduction

The Swedish government announced its intention in its budget proposal to parliament for 2007 to submit a White Paper on Swedish relations with Africa. The previous White Paper on this subject, 'Africa on the Move', was submitted in March 1998, with a revised and shorter version appearing in 2002. The White Paper is intended as the basis for the formulation of Swedish government policies towards Africa, not only regarding development cooperation but also in trade, security, cultural exchange and other areas of particular Swedish interest. Work on the new White Paper commenced in spring 2007, with the first draft to be available by 1 November 2007 and anticipated final submission by December 2007. The project is coordinated by the Africa Department of the Ministry for Foreign Affairs.

The White Paper will highlight new developments in Africa as well as other trends of relevance to Swedish relations with the continent. It will explore how these trends affect Sweden and how Sweden can position itself in relation to them. It will discuss those changes relevant not only to Swedish bilateral relations with Africa but also to Swedish involvement in EU and UN initiatives. Its point of departure will be the existing Swedish policy on global development. The White Paper is to focus on sub-Saharan Africa (SSA) as a whole and will not describe developments in individual African countries or sub-regions other than for purposes of illustration *(Holmberg, 2007)*.

The background material for the White paper consists of five papers, and the present paper deals with economic issues. The purpose is to put the African economy in a global perspective by showing its past developments relative to other regions. Throughout this paper, Africa is taken to mean sub-Saharan Africa. We start by looking at the growth and relative size of the African economy as well as its structure and trade patterns (Section 2). Then we identify the size and composition of financial flows to Africa and relate those to investment levels (Section 3). A heated debate has arisen over the increasing influence in Africa of Asian economies, and we complement the general discussion in Sections 2 and 3 with a specific discussion of the impact of 'the Asian drivers' (Section 4). Thereafter, we evaluate the effects of recent debt rescheduling initiatives on debt levels and domestic space to manoeuvre (Section 5). Then we review the major growth factors and impediments to growth in Africa (Section 6). In Sections 7–9 we look in greater detail at the links between HIV/AIDS, gender relations and the brain drain and economic growth. Section 10 discusses the effect on African trade of increased trade liberalisation and the potential effects of the proposed EPAs, while Section 11 discusses the role of principal internal and external economic actors. Section 12 provides a summary and draws some conclusions for Sweden. This is clearly a tall order for a short paper, but we will at least provide some comment on the relevant areas.

2.Comparative performance of the African Economy

Most African countries gained independence in the early 1960s, and the first decade thereafter saw quite rapid economic growth. From about the time of the first oil crisis in 1973, however, economic imbalances emerged. For a period, African economies tried to avoid economic adjustments by putting control regimes in place, but by the early 1980s the external deficits had become so severe that donors and other financiers were no longer willing to continue to provide support. Therefore, almost all African countries entered into a period of extensive economic reform known as structural adjustment, which aimed at bringing about both macroeconomic stabilisation and structural market-oriented economic reforms. This process was financed by structural adjustment loans from the Bretton Woods institutions, which were combined with extensive conditions to ensure that loan-receiving countries changed their policies in accordance with the agreed agenda. This process was politically controversial and there were numerous policy reversals and setbacks in the reform process. During the period up to 1995, some countries saw improvements in their per capita income levels, but most did not (Easterly, 2001). Still, most African economies achieved a measure of economic stabilisation with improvements in budget balance, monetary policy control, liberalisation of the foreign exchange market, and implemented a range of structural reforms such as privatisation of many state-owned firms. There was considerable variation in the pace and seriousness of reforms, though.

After a period of falling per capita incomes that started in the 1970s, there was finally a turn-around in about1995 (earlier for some countries of course), with on average modestly increasing per capita incomes. The last few years have actually seen average per capita incomes in Africa grow by more than 3% per year on average, partly due to the resource boom but also due to improved economic policies. In this section, we try to put this development in perspective by comparing it with that of other major regions.

In comparing a region's external economic links and relative position versus other regions, one can view the subject from two angles. One can look at Africa's relative importance in the world or one can look at how important the links with the world are to Africa. We will look at Africa from both these perspectives. By doing so we see that Africa is not very important for the world economy, while the world economy is very important to Africa.

We start by showing the current relative economic standard of the major regions of the world. Sweden together with the rest of the OECD and other rich countries are in the high income category.

TABLE 1 : REGIONAL POPULATION AND GDP SHARES AND RELATIVE INCOME LEVELS 2005

	Population share (%)	GDP share (%)	Relative GDP per capita World=100	Relative GDP per capita (PPP) World=100
High income *	15.7	78.8	495	343
East Asia & Pacific	29.3	6.8	23	64
Europe & Central Asia **	7.3	4.9	67	98
Latin America & Caribbean	8.6	5.5	64	88
Middle East & North Africa	4.8	1.4	30	64
South Asia	22.8	2.3	10	33
Sub-Saharan Africa	11.5	1.4	12	21

* All countries in which 2005 GNI per capita was US$10,726 or more, largely OECD countries, including Sweden.
** The old Eastern Bloc, excluding high income states.
Source: WDI 2007

We see in Table 1 that the high income countries still dominate, while Africa is a very small player in the global economy. At current exchange rates, Africa produced only 1.4% of global GDP in 2005 and had an average per capita income that was $^{1}/_{41}$ of that of the high income countries. If we adjust for differences in purchasing power (PPP estimates), which is appropriate when we want to compare living standards, the gap shrinks to 1/16, which is still enormous. In PPP-terms, Africa is clearly the poorest region in the world with an income level of about 2/3 that of South Asia, which is the second poorest region.

Thus, Africa stands out as the poorest region in the world. The next question is whether Africa is catching up or slipping further behind. The per capita income growth rates since 1961 in the regions of the world are shown in Table 2. We see here that Africa had a lower growth rate than the high income countries during the whole period 1961–2000. Since the turn of the century, however, it has grown faster than the rich countries, and this means that the relative gap has declined somewhat. This is promising, but there have been growth accelerations in Africa before which have petered out. The question is whether this one can be sustained and even accelerated. We note that particularly the Asian countries (with a few exceptions) have done extremely well, and for an extended period they have been growing faster than the rich countries, thereby reducing their income gap relative to the high income countries significantly.

TABLE 2: ANNUAL PER CAPITA INCOME GROWTH 1961–2005 (% PER YEAR)

	1961–70	1971–80	1981–90	1991–2000	2001–05
High income	4.1	2.6	2.4	1.9	1.4
East Asia & Pacific	2.5	4.5	5.8	7.1	7.3
Europe & Central Asia	-	-		-0.9	5.1
Latin America & Caribbean	2.6	3.2	-0.9	1.7	1.0
Middle East & North Africa	2.8	2.3	0.0	1.8	2.1
South Asia	2.0	0.7	3.4	3.2	4.7
Sub-Saharan Africa	2.3	0.8	-1.0	-0.3	2.0
World	3.3	1.9	1.4	1.4	1.5

Source: WDI 2007

Africa is of course a very diverse economic continent, with large differences across countries in their economic and political experiences. To nuance the picture, we provide further information about growth experiences by country (Table 3). A factor that has hampered growth in several African countries in recent decades is internal conflict or even outright war.

To be able to give at least some sense of the importance of conflict for growth, we have selected the growth histories of all countries that have been involved in significant violent conflict at some time since 1990. We have identified 16 such countries in sub-Saharan Africa. We present growth numbers for the full period since 1961, but have not differentiated further with regard to the timing of the conflicts.

In the same table, we also provide growth numbers for the current major recipients of Swedish aid. We simply chose the countries that received at least SEK100 m in 2006. In this group of 14 countries, there are six that are also in the category of conflict-ridden countries. Aid to such countries is of course often humanitarian, which is generally not primarily focused on growth.

Looking at Table 3, we first note that the countries receiving much Swedish aid today generally did badly in the 1980s, somewhat better in the 1990s, while many have been doing very well since the turn of the century. The average growth in per capita income per year for the main recipients of Swedish aid 2001–05 is 2.2%, which is slightly better than the sub-Saharan African average of 2%. The experiences range from high growth countries like Mozambique, Tanzania and Sudan (because of oil and in spite of conflict), to Zimbabwe, which is an unmitigated disaster under Mugabe with a decline in per capita income by over 6% per year.

TABLE 3: PER CAPITA INCOME GROWTH RATES 1961–2005 FOR MAJOR RECIPIENTS OF SWEDISH AID AND FOR COUNTRIES THAT HAVE BEEN INVOLVED IN ARMED CONFLICT, 1990 AND LATER

Major recipients of Swedish aid in 2006 (At least SEK 100 m)	1861–1970	1971–80	1981–90	1991–2000	2001–05
Burkina Faso	1.13	1.18	0.77	1.20	1.83
Congo, DR (Conflict)	0.43	-2.54	-2.04	-8.12	1.17
Ethiopia (Conflict)	*	*	-0.98	0.38	3.03
Kenya	1.30	4.28	0.37	-0.83	1.35
Malawi	2.26	2.97	-2.00	1.70	0.44
Mali	*	1.59	-1.61	1.32	3.27
Mozambique (Conflict)	*	*	-0.53	2.36	6.72
Rwanda (Conflict)	0.22	2.25	-1.05	1.27	2.91
South Africa	3.48	1.12	-0.91	-0.41	2.44
Sudan (Conflict)	-0.77	0.71	0.00	3.29	4.23
Tanzania	*	*	*	0.09	4.79
Uganda (Conflict)	*	*	-0.12	3.50	2.08
Zambia	0.68	-1.96	-2.14	-1.66	2.99
Zimbabwe	2.98	-0.12	0.70	-0.63	-6.17
Other countries that have been in conflict since 1990					
Angola	*	*	-0.61	-1.38	7.46
Burundi	2.93	0.79	1.28	-3.18	-0.85
Chad	-0.93	-3.86	2.78	-0.49	9.93
Congo, Rep.	1.36	3.35	1.84	-1.64	1.29
Eritrea	*	*	*	2.88	-0.66
Guinea-Bissau	*	-1.76	2.54	-0.87	-3.07
Liberia	2.06	-1.10	-10.55	3.82	-4.73
Senegal	-0.69	-0.82	0.26	0.33	2.26
Sierra Leone	2.44	0.47	-1.32	-5.26	9.39
Somalia	-1.00	-1.81	1.59	*	*

Note: Countries are defined as conflict countries if they have been involved in war in the 1990s or later or in a conflict that has cost more than 1,000 lives since it started. Information is taken from UCDP/PRIO (2007) – Armed Conflict Dataset 1946–2005.
Source: WDI (2007)

In our group of conflict countries, we see a few cases of very rapid growth. In Chad and Angola, this is driven by the boom in oil, while Sierra Leone has bounced back from a huge income
decline during the conflict. Burundi, Eritrea, Guinea-Bissau and Liberia continue to experience
falling per capita incomes. Clearly, civil war has been an important cause of bad economic performance in Africa, and the elimination of remaining conflicts as well as maintenance of peace
is obviously very important for progress in poverty reduction. There is by now an extensive
literature relating civil wars to the economy, which shows that bad economic performance is one
important cause of civil strife (see e.g., Collier, Hoeffler, 2004; Collier, 2007; Mlambo, Kamara,
Nyende, 2007).

One important aspect of development is the structural change that economies undergo as
they grow. Typically, one finds that the share of agriculture declines, while industry and services
expand. We also see such a pattern in Africa, where the share of agriculture in total output fell
from 29% in 1960 to 17% in 2005 (Table 4). The bulk of the labour force is still in agriculture,
though. We note that the share of industry grew until 1980, but then started to decline, being
replaced by services as the expanding sector. This indicates that the industrial sector, including
manufacturing, has not been able to expand as hoped at independence, or as it did in Asia. The
import-substitution policy that was pursued to support manufacturing growth in Africa achieved
some results in the 1960s, when there were manufacturing imports that could easily be replaced
by domestic production. However, once the easy substitutions were achieved, the scope for further growth was limited by the growth of domestic demand, since the policies had not led to the
creation of a manufacturing sector that could compete internationally. Import substitution was
clearly not the basis for an economic take-off like the one that happened in Asia.

TABLE 4: SECTORAL VALUE ADDED AS % OF GDP IN AFRICA 1960–2005

	1960	1965	1970	1975	1980	1985	1990	1995	2000	2005
Agriculture	29.3	25.9	22.3	21.4	18.7	20.1	19.6	19.3	18.3	16.7
Industry	26.8	28.6	28.7	32.1	37.8	33.8	33.7	31.4	31.3	31.8
Services, etc	44.6	45.5	49.0	46.5	43.5	46.1	46.9	49.3	50.4	51.6

Source: WDI 2007

Table 5 shows how the distribution of world exports has changed since 1961. We see here
that the share of the high income countries peaked in 1990, but that it has fallen dramatically since then. These lost shares have been taken over by the rapidly expanding East Asian
economies such as China, and recently also by the former Eastern Bloc that is making a
comeback on the world market. The African story has been a sad one. In 1960, sub-Saharan
Africa supplied as much as 4.2% of world exports, but by the turn of the century this had
shrunk to only 1.4%. (It is noteworthy that South Asia had an even smaller share at that time
and even today due to India's isolationist policies.) By 2005, however, sub-Saharan Africa
has increased its global market share somewhat due to the boom in natural resources such
as oil, and this is of course also one of the reasons for the growth acceleration. The bulk of
African exports are raw materials, agricultural products and tourism services. There is still no
breakthrough in terms of manufacturing exports.[1]

---

1. For reviews of the evidence in manufacturing development in Africa, see Bigsten and Söderbom (2006, 2007)

TABLE 5: EXPORT SHARES 1960–2005

	1960	1965	1970	1975	1980	1985	1990	1995	2000	2005
High income	75.1	76.8	79.3	78.1	77.7	77.8	81.4	80.2	77.7	72.3
East Asia & Pacific			2.2	2.6	3.5	3.8	4.1	6.5	7.7	10.2
Europe & Central Asia							6.0	5.0	4.9	7.0
Latin America & Caribbean	6.1	5.8	4.7	4.3	4.5	5.0	4.0	4.3	5.3	5.0
Middle East & North Africa		2.3	2.5	4.8	3.7	3.3	2.1	1.6	1.8	2.3
South Asia	2.2	1.7	1.1	0.8	0.7	0.8	0.8	0.9	1.1	1.5
Sub-Saharan Africa	4.2	4.0	3.3	3.0	3.5	2.3	1.8	1.4	1.4	1.7

Source: WDI 2007

It is clear that Africa is of marginal importance in world trade, which is not surprising when we consider that it produces only a marginal share of world output. However, if we reverse the perspective and check how important the world is for Africa, we get a radically different picture (Table 6). We see that until the 1990s Africa was more dependent on world market demand than East Asia, and it still is much more dependent on the world market than the high income countries (less so than Sweden, though, which exports 49% of GDP.) What the rich countries do with regard to trade with Africa is therefore very important for Africa's economic future. In 2005, 70.3% of African exports went to the developed countries (30.5% to Europe, 31.6% to the US), 13.3% went to Asia and only 9.4% was exported within Africa. The latter figure is surely underestimated, since there is also extensive unrecorded trade between African neighbours.

TABLE 6: EXPORTS OF GOODS AND SERVICES AS SHARES OF GDP 1960–2005

	1960	1965	1970	1975	1980	1985	1990	1995	2000	2005
High income	11.8	12.0	14.0	17.2	19.3	19.5	18.7	20.5	23.7	24.5
East Asia & Pacific	..	..	7.7	10.3	16.9	15.2	24.4	29.4	36.1	45.9
Europe & Central Asia	..	..	..	..	..	..	23.7	31.0	40.6	41.1
Latin America & Caribbean	10.8	10.3	9.9	11.0	13.2	16.1	17.0	18.8	20.8	25.8
Middle East & North Africa	..	21.1	24.1	34.4	29.8	20.0	24.4	26.5	28.4	37.1
South Asia	6.4	5.2	5.1	6.9	7.7	6.6	8.6	12.5	14.7	20.0
Sub-Saharan Africa	25.5	24.2	21.9	25.4	31.9	28.3	27.2	28.6	32.1	32.7
World	12.0	12.1	13.4	16.5	18.8	18.9	19.0	21.1	24.6	26.1

Source: WDI 2007

The level of per capita income is only one indicator of the standard of living, and to broaden the picture somewhat we can look at life expectancy. We see in Table 7 that Africa also stands out here. Life expectancy is lower in Africa than anywhere else, and we note that it even fell in the 1990s. This was generally not due to the economic problems but to the impact of HIV/AIDS (we revert to this issue below.) The simple point to make here is that even if one considers indicators other than income (we could have chosen others), Africa stands out as the region of the world that has the lowest standard of living

TABLE7: LIFE EXPECTANCY AT BIRTH 1960–2005

	1960	1970	1980	1985	1990	1995	2000	2005
High income	68.8	70.8	73.6	74.8	75.9	76.7	78.0	79.0
East Asia & Pacific	38.9	59.1	64.4	66.2	67.2	68.1	69.1	70.7
Europe & Central Asia	..	67.4	67.5	68.4	69.2	67.7	68.7	69.2
Latin America & Caribbean	56.3	60.4	64.6	66.4	68.1	69.9	71.2	72.5
Middle East & North Africa	47.2	52.6	58.3	61.6	64.3	66.4	68.1	69.6
South Asia	43.9	48.9	53.7	56.2	58.7	60.9	62.6	63.5
Sub-Saharan Africa	40.6	44.6	48.1	49.3	49.2	47.8	46.1	46.7
World	50.4	59.1	62.6	64.1	65.2	65.9	66.7	67.6

Source: WDI 2007

To conclude this section, we note that Africa is not only the poorest region of the world, but that it also has an increasing share of the world population. We see in Table 8 that the overall population growth rate in the world is consistently declining. The rate is going down in Africa as well, but since the region is lagging behind economically, it has not come as far as the other regions in the demographic transition process. The result is that sub-Saharan Africa's share of world population over a 45-year period has increased from 7.4% to 11.5%.

TABLE 8: POPULATION GROWTH RATE 1960–2005

	1960	1965	1970	1975	1980	1985	1990	1995	2000	2005
High income	*	1.19	1.07	0.96	0.83	0.67	0.84	0.96	0.81	0.72
East Asia & Pacific	1.98	2.43	2.72	1.93	1.50	1.55	1.62	1.26	0.92	0.85
Europe & Central Asia	1.67	1.33	0.91	1.03	0.95	1.00	0.65	0.11	-0.41	0.06
Latin America & Caribbean	2.84	2.75	2.56	2.44	2.28	2.08	1.84	1.67	1.50	1.32
Middle East & North Africa	2.57	2.65	2.70	2.81	3.03	3.09	3.38	2.10	1.90	1.85
South Asia	1.95	2.39	2.40	2.38	2.46	2.10	2.14	1.97	1.83	1.60
Sub-Saharan Africa	2.44	2.54	2.67	2.86	3.11	2.93	2.88	2.63	2.49	2.25
World	3.31	2.06	2.10	1.88	1.77	1.68	1.72	1.48	1.26	1.19

Source: WDI 2007

3. Financial flows to Africa

A key aspect of the process of globalisation is the ever closer financial integration of the world economy. This also affects Africa, but it is the region that is least integrated financially with the rest of the world and within the continent itself. We will here consider the role of capital markets and financial flows in the African growth process.

Economic growth requires investments, and investments are financed by savings. Those can be domestic savings or international savings transferred to the country. We first look at domestic savings (Table 9) and see that the African region saved 17.6% of GDP in 2005. At the other extreme we have East Asia, mainly China, which saved an astonishing 42.9%. The rapid growth of China is strongly related to these savings, and the relatively much poorer African growth performance is related to the low rate of saving (among other things).

TABLE 9: GROSS DOMESTIC SAVINGS (% OF GDP)

	1960	1965	1970	1975	1980	1985	1990	1995	2000	2005
High income	..	24.5	25.7	23.3	23.7	22.2	22.6	21.9	21.5	19.9*
East Asia & Pacific	32.8	24.3	26.2	28.3	33.2	31.8	36.2	39.6	35.8	42.9
Europe & Central Asia	..	..	..	..	..	..	25.8	22.4	23.8	23.5
Latin America & Caribbean	19.9	21.4	21.3	23.0	23.0	23.5	21.6	20.5	20.2	24.0
Middle East & North Africa	..	22.9	24.8	26.5	24.3	18.8	18.8	21.7	25.9	27.2
South Asia	12.1	13.5	13.5	14.7	13.3	18.1	19.9	22.9	22.4	26.0
Sub-Saharan Africa	17.5	18.7	19.6	21.5	25.9	20.2	18.8	16.2	19.1	17.6
World	22.9	23.9	25.0	23.3	23.8	22.6	23.2	22.7	22.3	21.4*

Note: Gross domestic savings are calculated as GDP less final consumption (total consumption). * = 2004.
Source: WDI 2007

Table 10 shows that capital formation in Africa is higher than domestic savings, which means that the difference is financed by some form of foreign saving. This can be in the form of foreign direct investment, loans, remittances or foreign aid.

TABLE 10: GROSS CAPITAL FORMATION (% OF GDP)

	1960	1965	1970	1975	1980	1985	1990	1995	2000	2005
High income	..	24.1	25.2	23.2	24.6	22.4	23.0	21.4	21.9	20.3
East Asia & Pacific	29.3	21.2	26.7	28.8	33.1	34.6	34.7	39.5	31.6	37.9
Europe & Central Asia	..	..	..	..	..	..	27.1	23.9	22.7	22.9
Latin America & Caribbean	20.4	20.6	21.8	25.4	24.5	19.1	19.3	20.9	21.0	21.1
Middle East & North Africa	..	21.8	22.6	30.5	29.4	26.0	28.0	24.6	23.8	25.8
South Asia	14.2	16.3	15.4	17.4	18.7	22.4	22.8	25.0	23.9	30.6
Sub-Saharan Africa	16.6	20.6	22.5	26.5	24.8	17.5	17.7	18.5	17.8	19.4
World	22.7	23.4	24.7	23.6	24.9	22.8	23.4	22.4	22.3	21.5

Source: WDI 2007

As a backdrop to the African picture, we note there has been an enormous increase in the magnitude of private financial flows to East Asia, although with a temporary setback at the turn of the century after the Asian crisis (see Appendix Table 1). Official transfers have shrunk to near insignificance, and the private flows are mainly made up of foreign direct investment. On the other hand, in the case of Africa official transfers still dominate, but there is a hopeful sign in the rapid increase of private flows in the last couple of years.

Figure 1 shows the evolution of three types of resource flows to Africa, namely official flows or aid, which was US$ 30.5 bn in 2005, foreign direct investments,[2] which were US$ 16.6 bn, and other private transfers, which includes various forms of private remittances, which were US$ 9.8 bn.[3] Particularly foreign direct investments have increased, mainly in the natural resource sector. The remaining private transfers, including remittances, have shown a steady increase.

Africa has not been very successful in attracting foreign private capital, although South Asia has been even less successful in this regard. The flows of aid to Africa can be seen as a response to the small size of private capital flows and of course a response the state of poverty in the region. Table 11 shows that Africa receives more aid per capita than any other major region, but not dramatically more than some of the other regions. However, if we look at aid inflows relative to GDP (Table 12) we see that Africa is by far the most aid-dependent region with aid inflows equivalent to 5.5 of GNI (with some relatively high figures in the Middle East as well for special reasons). There are a few countries with extremely high ratios in 2005 such as Burundi (47%), Congo (37%), Eritrea (37%), Liberia (54%), Malawi (28%), Rwanda (27%), Sao Tome and Principe (47%) and Sierra Leone (30%) (WDI, 2007). These are essentially countries that have come out of civil war and internal conflict and are in a rebuilding phase, and it is not unreasonable to argue that the need for aid (and usefulness of aid) is particularly high in those circumstances (Collier, 2006). Among more stable African countries, we have high inflows into major Swedish aid recipients such as Uganda (14%), Zambia (14%), Tanzania (12%), Mozambique (21%) and Ethiopia (17%). To some extent, these high numbers reflect debt write-offs but more so the fact that these countries have gradually done better economically and have become 'donor-darlings'.[4]

There has been concern that high aid inflows lead to lower tax collection efforts, and there are probably such effects. However, many countries have by now established semi-autonomous tax revenue authorities that can hire staff on much more generous terms than the regular civil service. These have in several instances shown considerable efficiency and been able to increase the tax revenue to GDP ratio. Still, generally the figure tends to be low, typically around 15% of GDP. Since public expenditures to GDP are mostly considerably higher, the difference is aid financed. This has been a cause of concern, but one should note that this is exactly the point of aid to the government! Aid is supposed to make possible higher spending on public services such as education, health, infrastructure etc. than what a government is able to collect in taxes. So it is a reasonable long-term goal to seek to increase tax collection, but one must keep in mind that taxable incomes in several countries are relatively low. Smallholders and the informal sector are hard to tax, so there is a risk that governments will try to tax the formal economy too much. Generally, it seems that tax laws are reasonable, but that efforts to implement them effectively are called for.

---

2. Foreign direct investment (net) shows the net change in foreign investment in the reporting country. Foreign direct investment is defined as investment that is made to acquire a lasting management interest (usually of 10% of voting stock) in an enterprise operating in a country other than that of the investor (defined according to residency), the investor's purpose being an effective voice in the management of the enterprise. It is the sum of equity capital, reinvestment of earnings, other long-term capital and short-term capital as shown in the balance of payments.
3. Private net resource flows are the sum of net flows on debt to private creditors plus net direct foreign investment and portfolio equity flows. Net flows (or net lending or net disbursements) are disbursements minus principal repayments.
4. Ethiopia has fallen from favour since 2005 because of the mishandling of the recent election.

FIGURE 1: OFFICIAL FLOWS, OTHER PRIVATE FLOWS (REMITTANCES), AND FDI IN SUB-SAHARAN AFRICA 1970–2005

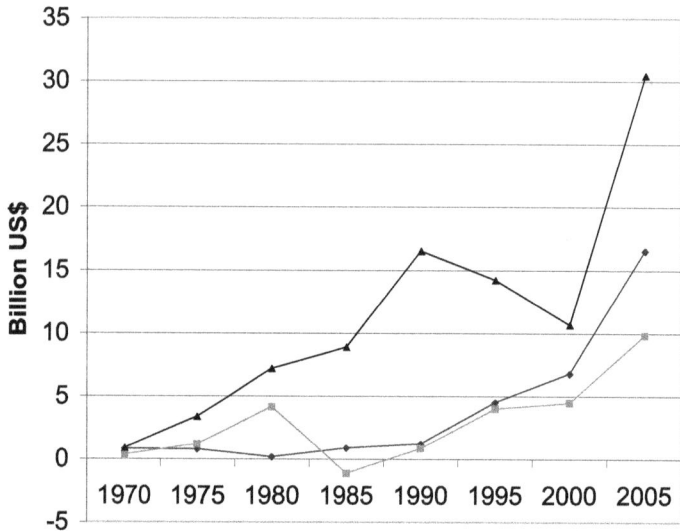

Source: Appendix Table 1.

TABLE 11 : AID ALLOCATION BY REGIONS 1960–2005 (CURRENT US$ PER CAPITA)

	1960	1965	1970	1975	1980	1985	1990	1995	2000	2005
High income	12.7	7.4	7.5	6.1	6.3	9.1	4.5	2.8	3.7	0.0
East Asia & Pacific	12.9	13.3	21.8	13.5	12.1	13.6	14.6	16.7	17.8	10.5
Europe & Central Asia	8.6	5.8	2.4	0.6	4.0	1.3	6.9	19.9	23.2	6.3
Latin America & Caribbean	5.2	14.3	15.5	8.4	7.5	11.8	9.6	10.7	10.0	7.0
Middle East & North Africa	21.0	9.7	13.9	28.4	24.8	16.9	19.6	9.4	9.4	29.8
South Asia	25.2	31.7	20.8	21.9	18.5	14.9	11.2	8.8	8.7	10.2
Sub-Saharan Africa	14.4	17.9	18.2	21.1	26.8	32.5	33.6	31.9	27.3	36.1

Source: WDI 2007

TABLE 12: AID AS % OF GNI 1960–2005

	1960	1965	1970	1975	1980	1985	1990	1995	2000	2004	2005
High income	0.1	0.0	0.0	0.0	0.0	0.0	0.0	0.0	0.0	0.0	0.0
East Asia & Pacific	0.6	0.8	1.1	0.9	0.9	0.8	1.2	0.8	0.5	0.3	0.3
Europe & Central Asia	..	..	..	..	..	..	0.3	1.1	1.1	0.7	0.2
Latin America & Caribbean	0.3	0.8	0.6	0.4	0.3	0.5	0.5	0.4	0.3	0.3	0.3
Middle East & North Africa	..	2.9	2.9	4.3	3.0	1.5	3.6	1.5	1.0	1.7	3.9
South Asia	2.4	2.6	1.7	2.6	2.3	1.4	1.5	1.1	0.7	0.8	0.9
Sub-Saharan Africa	2.0	2.6	1.9	2.6	2.9	4.5	6.2	6.1	4.1	5.3	5.5
World	0.3	0.3	0.2	0.3	0.3	0.3	0.3	0.2	0.2	0.2	0.2

Source: WDI 2007

Has aid to Africa been effective? The results of the research on the issue were reviewed in a recent issue of the Swedish Economic Policy Review. Tarp (2006) provides a comprehensive review of attempts to measure the impact of foreign aid. It must be noted that to make valid inferences, the evaluator needs to establish a proper counterfactual, and this requires assumptions that may be debatable.[5] Much of the evidence from project evaluations has shown the return on projects to be high on average, while doubts have remained about the overall growth impact. The latter concern has during the last decade been addressed in a series of studies trying to measure aid effectiveness. Analysts have mainly used a cross-country panel-data approach, which makes it possible to control for a whole range of variables. Centre stage in the late 1990s was the result from the study by Burnside and Dollar (2000), showing that although aid does not work in general, it works in good policy environments. However, several authors have found this result to be fragile. The most recent studies find that there is a significantly positive effect of aid on growth, although they are less positive in the tropics (and many African countries are in this category). Tarp concludes his review with the observation that the most common result in the literature is that aid has a positive effect on per capita income growth.[6] He also notes that this is not conditioned on good policies, although good policies of course make outcomes better.

Private remittances to Africa have shown an increasing trend according to official statistics, but there are also significant flows that are not recorded. Freund and Spatafora (2005) estimate that the informal flows are about half of the formal flows. On average, the remittances to Africa are about 2.5% of GDP, which is considerably less than flows to other developing countries, which are about 5% of GDP. The flows vary a lot between countries, with a migrant economy such as Lesotho receiving remittances corresponding to 28% of GDP (Gupta, Pattillo and Wagh, 2007).

One important positive feature of remittance incomes is that the flow has been rather stable, while both aid and FDI have fluctuated considerably. Remittances are also the positive side of the brain drain and have a poverty-mitigating effect. It is furthermore shown by Gupta, Pattillo and Wagh (2007) that the flows, apart from helping families to increase consumption, contribute to financial development. They provide an opportunity for low-income households to access formal financial services. This may start with savings, but over time it can lead to access to small-business start-up capital. If one could increase and formalise these flows by making formal transfer channels cheaper, they could help more with the integration of poor families into the formal financial market. Steady flows can help them secure small business loans, which can be invested for future growth.

---

5. We don't have any technique to construct a counterfactual that makes it possible to estimate properly what would have happened to Africa if aid had not been given at all.

6. In the same volume of the *Swedish Economic Policy Review*, Paul Collier (2006) summarises his reading of the literature on aid and growth in Africa as follows: "On my assessment, the econometric evidence is most consistent with the hypothesis that without aid Africa would have experienced absolute decline. For example, taking the recent study of Clemens et al. (2004) as an example, using the coefficients estimated in that study the scale of past aid to Africa would imply that it has raised the growth rate by something between one and two percentage points. This is quite a solid study, but it is towards the top end of the range of estimates. As Doucouliagos and Paldam (2006) note, generally aid seems to be less effective in the growth process in Africa than elsewhere. My own sense of the likely numbers is that over the long term the contribution of aid to African growth has been of the order of one percentage point per year. If this is accepted it has a disturbing implication: although with aid Africa has barely grown, without aid it would have experienced severe cumulative decline. Over the long term, aid has probably been decisive in keeping many economies afloat, even if it has not managed to transform them. Were Africa around 25% poorer than it is today, its problems would be correspondingly more severe". Collier also acknowledges that aid actually can do harm and that the donor community faces challenges with regard to their handling of the increased flows that are in the pipeline.

4. The Asian drivers

One of the most debated aspects of the current process of globalisation is the increase in trade between sub-Saharan Africa and Asia, particularly China and India. African exports to Asia have grown by over 10% per year from the early 1990s to 2003, which is twice as much as the growth of exports to the EU and the US (Subramanian, Matthijs, 2007). Recent growth rates are even higher, and during 2006 trade with China increased by 40% (Business Report, 2007). These numbers are evidence of a structural shift from North-South to South-South trade, but Asia's share of African exports is still only 13–14% (UN Comtrade, 2007).

In parallel with increasing trade, Chinese FDI has risen fast. This was US$ 20 m per year in the early 1990s, rose to almost US$ 100 m in 2000 and was over US$ 1 bn in 2006 (Zafar, 2007). Still, since total FDI was over US$ 30 bn per year, the Chinese role is still relatively limited. Currently, close to 700 Chinese state companies have invested particularly in oil, mining, fishing and telecommunications, but there are also substantial investments in roads, transport infrastructure and power generation. Moreover, Chinese companies have been setting up plants to circumvent quota regimes for textiles and clothing in the West (Subramanian, Matthijs, 2007).

The increased interaction between Africa and Asia obviously contains both threats and opportunities for sub-Saharan Africa. We note that sub-Saharan Africa mainly exports oil, mineral and precious metals, while it imports manufactured goods, mainly consumer goods. Table 13 highlights this by showing the top ten exports and imports. Crude oil, diamonds, platinum and gold make up almost 50% of Africa's exports to China, and seven of the import goods are manufactured products. Almost all imports are cheap consumer and capital goods, while there is little trade in intermediate goods.

TABLE 13. SUB-SAHARAN AFRICA'S TRADE WITH CHINA: TOP 10 EXPORTS AND IMPORTS

Exports to China		Imports from China	
Crude oil	37.0%	Ships and boats	4.0%
Diamonds	6.0%	Passenger motor cars	3.5%
Platinum	3.0%	Motor vehicle parts	2.4%
Gold	2.0%	Medicaments	2.3%
Coal	2.0%	Crude oil	2.0%
Cocoa Beans	2.0%	Radios	1.4%
Motor cars	2.0%	Cotton fabrics	1.3%
Ferro-alloys	1.5%	Rice	1.2%
Aluminium	1.3%	wheat	1.1%
Cotton	1.2%	Electric appliances	0.9%

Source: Subramanian and Matthijs (2007).

This kind of trade pattern has not in the past been conducive to sustainable economic growth. There are two problems. First, a natural resource boom is difficult to handle for countries with weak institutions, and there is a risk of domestic conflict, or at least gross misallocation of government income resources, i.e., it can become a resource curse. Second, imports of cheap manufactured goods are a threat to Africa's emerging manufacturing sector. This particularly affects textiles and clothing, and in several countries local firms are already struggling to survive (Kaplinsky, Morris, 2006).

China influences the terms of trade, raising prices for oil and minerals relative to agricultural commodities. This is a positive development for some countries, unless the resource curse sets in, but it is negative for others. When combined with the concentration of trade on a few countries, i.e., more than 75% of China's trade is with Angola, Nigeria, South Africa and Sudan, the impact of China's trade with sub-Saharan countries varies greatly across countries. In the short to medium run, there are some clear winners, resource-rich countries that export oil and base metals. And there are losers, countries that import oil and export agricultural commodities and textiles. Examples of winners are Angola, Gabon and Mozambique, and losers are Côte d'Ivoire, Kenya, Madagascar and Mauritius (Zafar, 2007).

There are also threats related to FDI. Chinese firms tend to invest in extractive industries with few links to local firms. They also use their own labour and do not invest much in African workers, although textiles and clothing is somewhat different. However, when Africa's advantage in the US market under AGOA ended in 2005, factories were closed down overnight (Zafar, 2007).

On the other hand, China's trade and investment in sub-Saharan Africa is an opportunity for economic growth and integration into the world economy. In many African countries, growth rates are higher than for decades (Tables 2 and 3), which no doubt is related to the commodity boom fuelled by China and to some extent India. Moreover, the increase in trade has made cheap consumer goods available to many Africans, thus raising living standards. And investments in production and infrastructure are bound to have beneficial effects both directly, through job creation and increased tax income, and indirectly, by improving the infrastructure for local firms.

Furthermore, China and India have huge and expanding consumer markets. There is scope for African firms to enter these markets: cut flowers, shrimps, pineapple, and other horticultural products are examples of products that could do well (Subramanian, Matthjis, 2007). Moreover, high quality coffee has a growth potential because of the low levels of consumption. Another sector is tourism. With rising middle classes in China and India, the tourism sector is expected to flourish. And, as an incentive to Chinese nationals, eight African countries were recently officially designated tourist destinations by the Chinese government (Business Report, 2007). An indirect effect of increased tourism is more direct flights and cheaper transport.

Sub-Saharan Africa is also benefiting from Chinese foreign aid. In 2006, China decided to double its aid to Africa by 2009, to form a US$ 5 bn fund for investments and promised to make US$ 3 bn of loans available over the next three years. Furthermore, China cancelled $US 1.4 bn of debt for 31 African countries (Business Report, 2007).

Not surprisingly, there are divergent views on the relative importance of the threats and opportunities facing sub-Saharan Africa. Kaplinsky and Morris (2006) are pessimistic and believe that de-industrialisation is almost inevitable. The only sources of hope are that the Asian economies will soon run into capacity constraints and rising costs, possibly due to labour shortages, or that their rapid economic growth generates a substantial appreciation in their currencies. Others are more optimistic, such as Broadman (2007), Subramanian and Matthjis (2007) and Zafar (2007). However, they underline the fact that the final impact is to a large extent determined by policies adopted both in sub-Saharan Africa and in China. Broadman (2007) suggests that China and India should eliminate escalating tariffs that limit Africa's exports, among other things.

Still, we should keep in mind that the direct Asian impact still is small relative to that of the Western industrialised economies, but since China and other countries in Asia are growing fast their relative importance will continue to increase. The African economies need to continue to reform to meet the challenge, for example by improving the functioning of markets. There is also a role for donors and international organisations in providing technical assistance and capacity building, mainly to strengthen trade-related institutions and improve policy implementation.

5. Impact of debt reduction initiatives

The success of debt reduction efforts depends on the ability of debtor countries to achieve high growth and foreign exchange earnings (Addison, 2006). This did not happen in sub-Saharan Africa in the 1980s and 1990s: so many countries were left with huge official debts after two decades of structural adjustment lending. Most highly indebted countries (relative to their GDPs) were therefore in Africa.

The HIPC programme was initiated by the World Bank and the IMF in 1996 and an extended version of it came into effect in 1999. The purpose was to reduce the debts of highly indebted countries to sustainable levels, that is a level at which they could service their debts. To gain access to this programme, the countries had to implement economic reform programmes. The plan was that the countries at the decision point, that is when they had completed the agreed upon reform process, would get a debt/export ratio not exceeding 150% and a debt/tax revenue ratio not exceeding 250%. Other debts are handled by the Paris Club, which provides debt reductions as part of debt clean-up operations. The Paris Club consists of governments with large outstanding debts in developing countries.

The HIPC programme led to some debt reduction, but many countries were left with debts they were unable to serve. The G8 proposal of June 2005, now called the Multilateral Debt Relief Initiative, therefore set out to cancel 100% of the debt that heavily indebted poor countries owed to the African Development Fund (AfDF), International Development Association and the International Monetary Fund. Complete debt reduction occurs when these LDCs have reached the completion point under the HIPC arrangement. This initiative is expected to result in a further reduction of debts by about US$ 50 bn. The MDRI does not propose parallel reduction of bilateral or commercial debt. The cancellation is contingent on sound macroeconomic performance, implementation of a Poverty Reduction Strategy and public expenditure management systems.

Debt relief has two major impacts. First, it influences the incentives for private investment. Second, it has a fiscal effect. The latter makes it possible to increase poverty-related expenditures. There are probably diminishing returns to debt relief as there are with regular aid. Recent political initiatives have tended to push the notion that debt relief is the preferred aid option, but one should always keep alternative uses of available aid money in mind. The long-term goal should not be to end debt forever, but to move countries to a sustainable debt position and to develop marketable debt instruments.

Still, the hope is that debt reductions will create more fiscal space for poor countries to finance poverty reduction measures. This will require good fiscal expenditure management as well as sound management of post-relief public borrowing. For the 29 countries that had benefited from debt relief by 2005, poverty related expenditures have increased from about 6% of GDP in 1999 to about 9% in 2005.

This is a significant improvement, but it should be noted that although extensive debt reductions in African countries have taken place, the reduction in actual debt service has been rather limited. Many countries did not service their debt properly. The 18 countries that had reached the completion point in 2006 (Benin, Bolivia, Burkina Faso, Ethiopia, Ghana, Guyana, Honduras, Madagascar, Mali, Mauritania, Mozambique, Nicaragua, Niger, Rwanda, Senegal, Tanzania, Uganda and Zambia) had only paid about US$ 1.5 bn per year in debt services. Still, it is important to get the debts off the books to facilitate policy making and eventually to become a regular borrower on the global financial market again. In the short term, however, the former HIPC-countries should avoid building up non-concessional debt.

Figure 2 shows how total sub-Saharan Africa debt has evolved over time. We see that the build up of the debt stock ceased in the mid-1990s and there has been a clear decline in total outstanding debt in the last few years. Table 14 shows that that actual debt service has declined, and this has increased the room for domestic expenditures.

It is not easy to measure how debt reduction has affected African growth rates, but it seems reasonable to assume that it has had some positive impact on investment incentives. It should have relieved the pressure of taxation (current and future) on investors and the general public. And it has increased the scope in budgets for both poverty oriented expenditures and growth-enhancing expenditures.

FIGURE 2: DEBT OUTSTANDING, TOTAL LONG-TERM (US$)

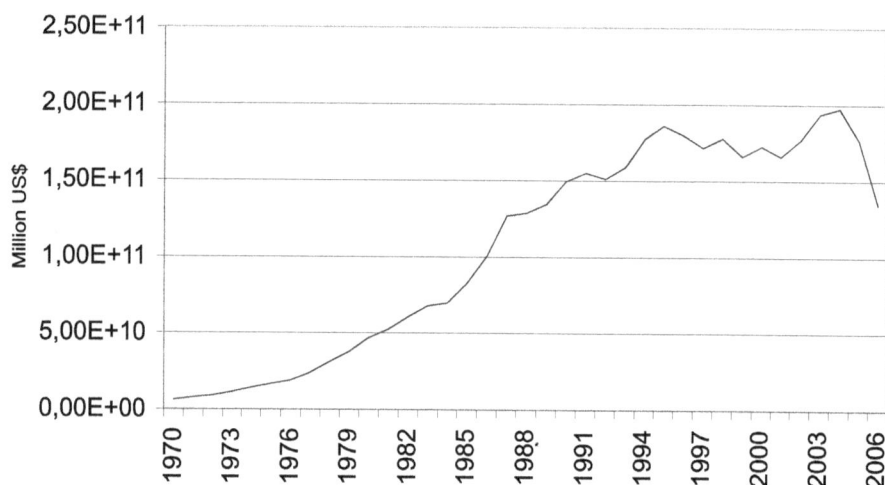

Source: Global Development Finance 2007.

TABLE 14: TOTAL DEBT SERVICE (% OF GNI)

	1970	1975	1980	1985	1990	1995	2000	2005
East Asia & Pacific	..	..	..	4.0	4.8	4.1	4.4	2.9
Europe & Central Asia	1.1	0.8	..	9.5	..	3.7	8.2	9.4
Latin America & Caribbean	3.2	3.4	6.5	7.3	4.2	4.9	9.4	6.8
Middle East & North Africa	..	..	4.5	3.8	6.4	6.9	4.7	3.9
South Asia	1.5	1.1	1.2	1.9	2.8	3.9	2.6	2.8
Sub-Saharan Africa	1.6	1.9	..	..	..	4.9	4.3	3.6

Source: WDI 2007

There are of course a range of problems related to debt cancellations. First, in all likelihood such cancellations mean de facto that aid resources are shifted from countries with better governance that have managed keep their debt under control and serviced to countries with poorer governance that have not done so. Another concern is what the signal for the future is. It may stimulate countries to borrow recklessly again expecting that somebody else will pick up the tab in the end. It is therefore important that one tries to ensure that the countries that get the debt relief actually undertake reforms that reduce the risk that money is squandered again.

6. Opportunities for and constraints on growth

a. Growth perspectives

There are several schools of thought on long-term economic development that can provide insights into what is needed for Africa to take off. Classical growth theory focuses on investment, technological change and the diffusion of technology. New institutional economics argues that countries must have appropriate institutions in place to be able to take advantage of new technologies. New economic geography (see e.g., Krugman, Venables, 1995) focuses on location and introduces distance into trade models to explain how growth spreads.

It is clear that investment and technological progress are necessary for growth, but the question is why growth outcomes have been so dramatically different in different parts of the world. There is a vast literature estimating reduced form regressions, where per capita incomes or growth of countries are regressed directly on various proxies for institutional quality, including political institutions. The estimated coefficients for the institutional variables measuring the security of property rights and constraints on the executive are generally highly significant (Hall and Jones, 1999; Acemoglu, Johnson, Robinson, 2001, 2002, 2003). It seems clear that the capacity to absorb and effectively implement new technology depends on domestic factors such as social capabilities, human capital and institutions. These may be regarded as the 'deeper' determinants of growth than investment.

So what hinders African countries from effective implementation of best practice policies and institutions? Institutionalists believe that the character of institutions and incentives is highly path dependent (North, 1990). The argument here is that network-externalities and vested interests hold back change, as do informal constraints in customs and traditions, which are hard to change through policy reforms. Elites may be reluctant to support policy reforms that give secure property rights if they make it possible for competing elites to emerge. The incumbent elite may choose to block certain investments for fear of losing political power if an independent economic elite evolves.

Crafts and Venables (2002) argue that most growth studies so far have underestimated the role of geography. They emphasise that size and distance are important determinants of development, and that agglomeration benefits dominate the process. The theory, as set out by Krugman and Venables (1995), aims to explain both agglomeration and dispersion of production. The starting point is that investment in a country is determined by a combination of internal factors and factors characterising the relationship to other countries. The domestic factors are factor endowments, skills, technology and social infrastructure. The international factors are access to world product markets and to suppliers of intermediate goods, factors of production and knowledge. When some countries take off and leave others behind, the wage gap will increase. When it has become large enough, there will be relocation of production from the centre towards parts of the periphery. The question of interest here is when Africa's turn will come.

So to sum up, factor accumulation and technological change are necessary for growth. The impact of investment and technology in turn depend on existing social capabilities, institutions and human capital. Societies with good organisation in terms of economic, social and political institutions that protect private property prosper. At the same time, we know that the organisation and institutions of society are hard to change, and particularly so for an outside agent such as an aid donor. We have also noted that the costs of economic interaction across distance affect the geographical distribution of economic activity. Thus, economic activity depends on internal capacity, but we must also take account of relationships with other countries. To take off, African countries need access to world markets and to external suppliers of goods, factors and knowledge.

b. The sustainability of growth

In the early cross-country regressions on growth, there was often an African dummy that was significantly negative. In recent work, however, this has generally been eliminated by the inclusion of relevant explanatory variables. Africa seems to grow more or less in the same fashion as other regions, but it rates poorly on many of the variables that determine growth (Hoeffler, 2002). Factors that are found to be robust explanations of Africa's poor growth are "expensive investment goods, low levels of education, poor health, adverse geography, closed economies, too much public expenditure and too many military conflicts" (Artadi, Sala-i-Martin, 2003:1; Tsangarides, 2005).

There is also a recent literature focusing not directly on the long-run growth patterns but on growth accelerations and the extent to which these can be sustained (Hausmann, Pritchett, Rodrik, 2004). Using this approach on African countries, Pattillo et al. (2005) find that growth tends to accelerate when policies and institutions improve. Growth episodes that are sustained for a decade or more are characterised by growth in trade and investment, low debt and democratic institutions. There is a strong link between institutional quality, policy stance and growth accelerations. Hausmann et al. found that economic liberalisation and democratisation were associated with sustained accelerations, while the effect of positive terms of trade shocks were not sustained. In conclusion, Pattillo et al. note that key factors supporting growth accelerations are trade, investment, productivity, policy and sound institutions. Pattillo et al. (2005) find that growth in sub-Saharan Africa would increase by 1.7 percentage points if the continent achieved the average world quality of institutions. They do not find any consistent association between geography or resource availability and growth episodes, though. They also find that the link between changes in political institutions and economic institutions is weak in sub-Saharan Africa.

c. Growth opportunities vs. constraints

The most ambitious attempt to explain variations in African economic growth has been undertaken by the African Economic Research Consortium (O'Connell, 2004; Collier, O'Connell, 2004). The project has attempted to identify the growth opportunities and constraints and to explain the success or failure of countries in seizing the opportunities. The study characterises opportunities for growth along two dimensions. The first dimension divides countries into three geographical categories, namely coastal countries, landlocked countries and resource-rich countries (irrespective of location). The second dimension is the degree of polarisation in the society, from not polarised to moderately polarised and highly polarised countries.

After defining the opportunities, the study goes on to investigate how domestic governments have shaped the growth environment in the various countries covered. Four different types of anti-growth syndromes are identified from the case studies. First, there is the regulatory syndrome, which refers to excessive government interventions in markets. Second, there is the redistributive syndrome, where efficiency-reducing resource transfers play a dominant role in government policy. Third, there is the intertemporal syndrome, which redistributes resources from the future to the present via, for example, looting by the elite or unsustainable government spending booms generally followed by sharp adjustments. Fourth, there are the state breakdown syndromes, in the form of civil war or severe political instability. Finally, there are also countries that are characterised as syndrome-free. The empirical analysis shows that an absence of syndromes increases the growth rate by almost 2% per year.

When looking globally at the performance of landlocked countries, Collier and O'Connell (2004) find strong evidence that resource-scarce landlocked economies have dramatically worse opportunities for growth and that there are two basic mechanisms behind this. First, being landlocked implies high constraints on market access, which has the effect of precluding manufactures from significant entry into the global market. Second, without high-value resources, landlocked countries are wholly dependent upon agriculture. There is no example of any such Third World country experiencing rapid growth during the period 1960–2000. The issue of geography is thus very important in the African context.

O'Connell notes that growth accelerations in Africa have often tended to evaporate. One reason is that growth in the early stages of the acceleration is not real. For example, most of the government component of GDP is measured at cost, and thus increases with the growth of government wages. Since government wages often exceed the opportunity cost of government workers, the resulting increase in measured real GDP is partly illusory. If the government expansion proves unsustainable, it is generally hard for the government to lay off workers and, instead, other types of expenditures will be cut with negative supply side effects. Overspending booms are therefore often followed by economic decline

The main conclusion of the African Economic Research Consortium study is that African growth has faltered due to poor governance. Africa's poor growth performance is not the product of a uniform phenomenon but due to the interaction of different types of governance failures with different effects, depending on the character of the constraints and opportunities in the specific country.

d. Poverty traps

An alternative characterisation of the African growth problem is found in Jeffrey Sachs et al. (2004), who argue that Africa is caught in a poverty trap. They argue that African countries will not be able to break out of the poverty trap unless large-scale foreign assistance is injected into the system. What is needed is an investment strategy alongside international changes in policies and governance structures.

Sachs does not accept the view that the poor African performance is due to poor governance. He argues that this is in itself an effect of poverty, and that poor countries are poorly governed because of lack of resources and skills. He argues that African countries are not more badly governed than other poor countries. Savings are needed to cover replacement investment, investment to compensate for population growth and finally investment to increase the capital stock. Since savings in Africa are low, the continent tends to get stuck in a low level of equilibrium. This is a classical argument from the early writings in development economics. What is needed, according to Sachs, is a big push in investment to get the economy to the point at which it can rise to the high level equilibrium. Sachs identifies three reasons for the poverty trap. First, savings are too low, since people are too poor to save enough. Second, they have many children. Third, capital has a threshold level below which it is not productive. Small savings are then not enough to increase the capital stock. At the macroeconomic level, poverty-trap models suggest that African countries need to attain a threshold income level and that they then will take off.

Critics of Sachs have pointed out that in a conventional growth model, countries experiencing a large negative shock should grow quickly once conditions change for the better, whereas in the poverty trap model they would stagnate. If financial resources were the binding constraint, African countries that have enjoyed persistent commodity booms should have leveraged those into an exit from the trap. This has not happened, but maybe the chance is better at present with a somewhat better policy regime in place.

e. Aid strategy and growth

Sachs agrees that the impact of geographical and bio-physical conditions needs to be taken into account. Transport costs are very high in Africa, since most of the population lacks access to waterways. Poor transport infrastructure means that producers cannot compete on the world market, at least not if imported inputs are required in production.[7] Sachs also notes that the continent is dry and sparsely populated, and the land is hardly irrigated at all and there is little use of fertiliser. The health situation in Africa is worse than anywhere else and life expectancy is low. Malaria is a huge problem, and AIDS has recently emerged as an enormous burden (see the detailed discussion in the next section). Sachs's conclusion is that what is needed for Africa is a large injection of foreign aid to finance national investment programmes based on domestic Poverty Reduction Strategies. Sachs et al. provide a programme to improve the preconditions for growth. The interventions focus on agriculture, health and education. A platform needs to be built in agriculture and human development.

What are the problems with this strategy? The starting point of the discussion was that Africa faces larger challenges than other regions. The demand on policy makers is larger than in other regions, at the same time there is a serious governance problem. In recent years, African economies have changed many of their policies in a sensible direction, but the problem of revamping the administrative machinery is a task of a much larger order. Implementation is a key problem in Africa. There are several studies that suggest that the main problem in Africa is not investment levels but returns on investment.[8] The main question concerning large aid injections is therefore how the new or expanded programmes are to be managed. How can one reach a situation where governments have incentives and possibilities to deliver efficient administration? Tight foreign control by donors in the form of policy conditionality has generally not worked well.

Sachs et al. assume constant state of the art efficiency in service delivery, or that absorptive capacity is not a problem. Critics have argued that they have underplayed both the uncertainties in his prescription and the constraints on an effective scaling-up of aid. The innovation in the Sachs paper is that it advocates a massive and externally funded scaling-up of a country's public service delivery. However, the central thrust of the recent literature on African development has been the dismissal of capital fundamentalism as a viable interpretation of Africa's way forward.

Pritchett and Woolcock (2004) point out that many of the MDG services are both trans-

---

7. Hulten (1996) finds that about a quarter of the difference in growth between sub-Saharan Africa and East Asia can be explained by differences in the effective use of infrastructure.
8. Dollar and Easterly (1999) estimated where Zambian income levels would have been with normal rates of returns on investments undertaken since independence. The difference is enormous!

action intensive and discretionary. Unlike many macroeconomic reforms, the delivery of many health and education services requires the collaboration of multiple individuals who make highly discretionary choices in an environment where many key actions are unobservable. Such services cannot be delivered by a few politically protected technocrats. They are subject to deep incentive problems. The empirical link between spending on health and education to outcomes is notoriously weak. The question about governance is not whether it is good relative to income levels, but whether it is good enough in absolute terms to be able to handle rapidly increased spending on public services without too many diminishing returns. Institutions need to be strengthened if they are to be able to manage increased aid flows effectively. There is, in any case, clearly a large scope for scaling-up donor activity in the broad area of science-intensive regional public goods, including basic research in health and agriculture. And debt relief is easily absorbed.

7. Impacts of HIV/AIDS

There is now ample evidence that HIV/AIDS has widespread consequences for both economic growth and economic development in general. Hence, the first sub-section reviews studies on the effects of HIV/AIDS on economic development, with an emphasis on per capita GDP growth. Economic measures, such as GDP per capita, are of interest because they show the impact of HIV/AIDS on average income, which matters to those surviving the epidemic. Moreover, they determine the amount of resources available to government for public expenditure on health, education, etc. Yet, it should be emphasised that economic measures are insufficient for evaluating living standards in the context of a full-blown AIDS epidemic, since they say little about the physical or mental wellbeing of the population.

In the following sub-sections, HIV/AIDS and human capital, gender, agricultural production and the public and private sectors are briefly discussed. More extensive reviews can be found in Barnett and Whiteside (2002), Casale (2005) and Arrehag et al. (2006).

During the last couple of years, the distribution of medicine to prevent the development of AIDS (anti-retroviral therapy) has expanded significantly in several countries. The availability of treatment is likely to have economic consequences, but so far there are few studies documenting the impact. Research discussed in this section is primarily based on data collected when a very small number of people were on anti-retroviral therapy.

a. HIV/AIDS: a constraint to economic development?

The African HIV/AIDS epidemic was detected in the early 1980s when the first AIDS cases were diagnosed in Congo, and by 1990 AIDS cases had been recorded in most countries (Hammarskjöld, 2004). Currently, about 25 million people in sub-Saharan Africa are infected with HIV and approximately 2.8 million became infected in 2006 (UNAIDS, 2006). HIV prevalence rates among adults vary greatly across countries: Swaziland has the highest adult prevalence, 33.4%, while HIV prevalence in Madagascar is well below 1%. However, in most parts of sub-Saharan Africa the HIV/AIDS epidemic is not only a health problem but a human disaster with far-ranging social and economic consequences.

Many studies have attempted to analyse the economic effects of the HIV/AIDS epidemic and several address the links between HIV/AIDS and economic growth. Nonetheless, there is still not a consensus on how the epidemic affects income per capita.[9] Studies from the early 1990s typically found that HIV/AIDS might reduce per-capita GDP growth, but that the impact would be modest. A representative study is Cuddington and Hancock (1994), which looked at Malawi. It predicted a fall in the growth rate of GDP of 0.2 percentage points, and that the impact on GDP per capita by 2010 would be negligible. The consequences of the epidemic would thus be so small that improved macroeconomic management could offset the negative macroeconomic effects.

In the models of the early 1990s, HIV/AIDS affects growth through three channels: it reduces the size of the labour force because of premature death; workers' efficiency declines because of bad health and loss of cumulative work experience; and savings decline because of increased health expenditure. The ultimate impact is determined by the decline in labour productivity and whether the amount of capital per worker increases or decreases. Over time, it has become clear that models developed along these lines tended to underestimate

---

9. For reviews of studies on the macroeconomics of HIV/AIDS, see Barnett and Whiteside (2002), Haacker (2004) and Casale (2005).

the impact of HIV/AIDS since important mechanisms were missing. Moreover, they failed to incorporate the rapid spread of the epidemic (Casale, 2005).

Several recent studies have obtained larger negative effects by using better data and more sophisticated models. Haacker (2002), analysing nine Southern Africa countries, finds that the rate of per capita output will be between 0.3 and 0.7 percentage points lower than without HIV/AIDS over the period 2000–10. In the long term, after 2010, there will be some recovery due to demographic changes. Bonnel (2000) gets a similar result in a cross-country study using African data: on average HIV/AIDS reduces Africa's per capita growth rate by 0.7 percentage points. Since the average per capita growth rate was 0.4% per year in the sample, this is substantial. Arndt and Lewis (2001), studying the South African economy, find a somewhat stronger effect: real GDP will be 20% lower in 2010 than if there had not been an HIV/AIDS epidemic. By means of a different approach, i.e., calibrating a dynamic model for a typical African economy, Corrigan, Glomm and Mendez (2005) obtain results similar to those of Arndt and Lewis (2001). Finally, McDonald and Roberts (2006), using panel data for a large number of countries, report that the average marginal impact on per capita income growth of a 1% increase in HIV prevalence rate is -0.59% in sub-Saharan Africa.

In spite of these findings, UNAIDS claim in their 2004 global report that the impact on GDP per capita is relatively small. This view is not completely unfounded, although UNAIDS does not seem to support it any longer.[10] For instance, Bloom and Mahal (1997) run cross-country regression and fail to find that HIV/AIDS affects GDP per capita growth. Werker, Ahuja and Wendell (2006) reach the same conclusion by making a serious attempt to control for the reverse causality in their statistical analysis, i.e., that low growth causes HIV/AIDS. An even more surprising result is obtained by Young (2005a, 2005b). By estimating and simulating models with micro data, he finds that the epidemic will be an economic boon for the survivors. This is caused by a decline in fertility which outweighs the negative effects of the fall in human capital.

Young's result hinges on the future evolution of the dependency ratio, defined as the number of children and elderly divided by the number of adults of working age. HIV/AIDS kills people of working age but it reduces fertility even more. The main reason for the decline in fertility is increased fear of infection, both for the woman herself but also for her offspring. As a result, HIV/AIDS is speeding up the decrease in the dependency ratio that is taking place in sub-Saharan Africa, a consequence that most other researchers had ignored. Young (2005b) provides support for the hypothesis that HIV/AIDS reduces fertility by analysing micro data from 27 sub-Saharan countries.

Lorentzen et al. (2005) and Kalemli-Ozcan (2006) have another view. They claim the main impact of HIV/AIDS will be through its effect on adult mortality. Adult mortality affects the time horizon people use when planning for the future. An increase in adult mortality makes people more myopic and thus reduces investment in both physical capital and education. In addition, it leads to higher fertility: families have more children when the uncertainty of survival of their offspring into adulthood is high. Hence, they argue that AIDS, by increasing adult mortality, has a strong negative impact on growth in per capita income. Both Lorentzen et al. (2005) and Kalemli-Ozcan (2006) provide evidence in favour of the hypothesis by analysing macro data for a number of countries.

As is evident, it is difficult to capture all the important mechanisms in a model and evaluate their relative impact. It is also hard to model nonlinear relationships correctly, yet they

---

10. In *UNAIDS/WHO AIDS Epidemic Update* 2006 the negative economic effects are clearly recognised.

are bound to be important. There is, for instance, no reason to believe that the impact of the disease increases monotonically when prevalence rises from 1% to 15% (McPherson, 2003). If there are important nonlinear relationships, the epidemic can cause large changes, such as a sudden implosion. Arrehag et al. (2006) and de Waal (2006) discuss various scenarios in which HIV/AIDS causes a widespread collapse at a national level.

Even if there is controversy over the impact on GDP per capita, most research seems to show that HIV/AIDS increases poverty and worsens income distribution. There are several factors indicating that the disease increases poverty beyond its macroeconomic effects. At the household level, the final impact depends on the availability of resources in the community and to the household. A low-income household without savings or access to loans has more difficulties in adjusting to an increase in expenditures and reduction in income caused by HIV/AIDS than others, and is likely to become even poorer (Barnett and Whiteside , 2002, Chapter 7).

In an innovative study, Salinas and Hacker (2006) simulate the impact of HIV/AIDS on poverty over a ten year period in four sub-Saharan countries using nationally representative survey data. The impact on per capita income varies depending on HIV prevalence in high-income population groups. However, even in cases where HIV/AIDS does not reduce per capita income, poverty increases. The size of the effect on poverty depends on how many people live near the poverty line and the prevalence rates among them. Salinas and Hacker (2006) show that HIV/AIDS causes the share of the population living with incomes below US\$ 1 per day to increase in line with HIV prevalence rates: for example, poverty increases by 10 percentage points in Swaziland, 6 percentage points in Kenya and 1.5 percentage points in Ghana. Besides, in these simulations the Gini coefficients rise in all countries. The largest impact is in Zambia, where it increases from 47.8% to 53.2%.

b. HIV/AIDS and human capital

The epidemic is also likely to have a negative influence on human capital and human knowledge in general. First, there is the direct effect when experienced or educated workers become ill or die. Second, both the quantity and quality of schooling are likely to decrease. Third, there is less parent-to-child transfer of knowledge.

There are several reasons to expect demand for education to decrease in severely affected countries. The opportunity cost of sending a child to school might increase, since the demand for labour and caregiving increases when a household member becomes ill. And the adverse impact on household income of having a member who is ill might reduce the share of the household budget allocated to children's schooling. Furthermore, the rapid increase in AIDS orphans, who are usually taken care of by relatives, also contributes to reduced demand for schooling. This is both for psychological and economic reasons. In countries with high prevalence rates, these factors are likely to lead to lower enrolment rates, increasing absenteeism and high repetition and dropout rates, particularly for girls.

In addition, there is the impact of life expectancy on the rate of return on education: reduced life expectancy is expected to lead to lower demand for education. This effect has been observed in several studies (Birdsall, Hamoudi, 2004; Lorentzen et al, 2005; Kalemli-Ozcan 2006). On the other hand, Young (2005a) suggests that the AIDS epidemic might lead to higher expected returns to education. The loss of educated prime-age adults should decrease the supply of educated labour, which could raise wages. The AIDS epidemic would then increase demand for education, something that Young argues could be taking place in South Africa.

Nonetheless, in most sub-Saharan countries the effect of changes in expected return to education seems more apparent than real. It probably has a very small, if any, impact on primary education, and there is usually severe rationing of secondary and tertiary education.

HIV/AIDS also affects the supply of education. AIDS increases attrition and absenteeism among teachers substantially. However, the extent of the problem is hard to estimate because of poor data and public-sector inefficiency unrelated to HIV/AIDS. Moreover, there is a negative impact on educational governance: mortality rates for managers, school inspectors, administrators and planning officials are often substantially higher than for teachers (Bennell, 2005).

Although it is difficult to pinpoint the size of the influence of HIV/AIDS on schooling, data from recent Malawi school censuses are indicative of a serious crisis. As many as 25% of the pupils repeat each grade in primary school, and after eight years at school about 60% of the pupils have dropped out. Another way of viewing the problem is that the Malawi government pays for the equivalent of 20 school years to get one student to complete his/her eight years of primary education (World Bank, 2004).

A recent study that evaluates the impact of HIV/AIDS on education in seven sub-Saharan African countries is Fortson (2006). She estimates the effect of local HIV prevalence on educational outcomes in the general population, not only on households with HIV-positive members or orphans. She finds that children living in areas with HIV prevalence rates of 10% complete about 0.5 fewer years of schooling than children living in areas without HIV. This is a substantial difference, since the mean years of schooling among adults is 4.7 years.

In the long term, the epidemic also has repercussions on human capital formation through another channel, the intergenerational transfer of human capital. In countries where the majority of the labour force works in subsistence farming, the middle generation's role in the knowledge transfer of farming practices is probably as important as formal education. Mtika (2003) explores the transfers of this sort of knowledge, and concludes that prime-age adults are crucial for intergenerational (between parents and children) and generational (between siblings) resource transfers. Moreover, the magnitude of such transfers is dependent on the health status of the individual. Hence, the long run impact on the productivity of human capital is likely to be much greater than it appears if educational attainment alone is considered. Bell et al. (2004) make a similar argument in a study of South Africa, emphasising that the intergenerational effect will continue long after the epidemic has peaked.

There are few studies that convincingly capture the long-run effects of HIV/AIDS on educational performance, due to lack of data. However, Beegle, de Weerdt and Dercon (2006) use data on a sample of initially non-orphaned Tanzanian children in 1991–94 and analyse the impact of observed orphanhood from ages 7 to 15 on educational attainment in 2004. They find that maternal orphans on average permanently lose almost one year of schooling. Since orphanhood is one of the direct consequences of HIV/AIDS (for example, in Zambia there are 710 000 AIDS orphans in a population of 11.6 million), this indicates a grim long-term impact of the disease (UNAIDS Fact Sheet, 2007 UNAIDS Fact Sheet, 2007, available at http://www.unaids.org/en/).

c. HIV/AIDS and gender

There is strong gender aspect to HIV/AIDS. Women constitute the majority of those who are HIV-positive (57% in sub-Saharan Africa), and the prevalence rates among those aged 15–24 are many times higher for females than for males. Women also carry a large part of the burden of HIV/AIDS: they take responsibility for the care of those who are ill, on top of a heavy workload. Moreover, when the husband passes away, they may lose their assets and may even be forced to move to their original home village. And those women that inherit the right to cultivate land often have difficulties in getting credit, obtaining services from extension workers, access to farm inputs, etc. Consequently, households that continue farming usually have much lower per capita income than when the husband was alive (Jayne et al., 2005).

d. HIV/AIDS and agricultural production

There has been extensive research on the impact of HIV/AIDS on agricultural production. However, most studies have been based on small samples or in just one village, making the findings highly tentative. A common result for small-scale farming is that AIDS creates labour shortages, and that the dominant method for coping with these is to switch from labour-intensive to less labour-intensive crops. In Eastern and Southern Africa, particular focus has been put on shifts from maize to roots and tubers and on reduction in labour-intensive cash crops such as tobacco, Irish potatoes, groundnuts and rice (Shah et al., 2002; Bollinger et al., 2000). Hence, high-value crops are replaced by low-value crops, and maize is replaced by the less nutritious cassava.

Using nationally representative longitudinal samples, recent research has questioned the concept of a homogenously affected household (Jayne et al., 2005). Responses to prime-age deaths seem to vary substantially across households and there are alternative ways of coping. In a study of Eastern and Southern African countries, Mather et al. (2004) fail to find a systematic shift towards less labour-intensive crops: households affected by prime-age deaths did not, on average, cultivate less remunerative crops than non-affected households. This is to some extent due to the fact that they do not uniformly have less labour than non-affected households: larger households are more likely to experience prime-age deaths. Another reason is that many households manage to attract new members or employ workers that replace the lost ones.

Nevertheless, the difference in income was very large for households that had experienced the death of the household head. For instance, in Malawi these households earned MK 17,500 (US$ 170) compared to MK 29,400 (US$ 280) for a non-affected household. On the other hand, households that had lost other prime-age adults had roughly the same income as non-affected households. Since about half of the affected households had lost the household head, these findings emphasise the fact that the impact of HIV/AIDS is to a large extent determined by who in the family is lost to AIDS. It is important not to treat all households affected by HIV/AIDS as identical, when, for example, providing social assistance for poverty alleviation.

Beegle, De Weerdt and Dercon (2007) also use a panel data set to analyse the impact on consumption of prime-age adult mortality in a rural area in Tanzania. They find that an affected household will experience a decrease in consumption of 7% within the first five years after the adult death. Since there is economic growth in the area, this creates a 19 percentage point growth gap to the average household. Again, this is a large effect since as many as 22% of the households experienced the death of an adult.

e. HIV/AIDS and the public and private sectors

No doubt the epidemic has a substantial impact on the public sector, since it primarily provides services, making labour and human capital the most important factors of production. Mortality leads to loss of labour and knowledge and causes attrition, which leads to more vacancies, partly for bureaucratic reasons and partly because there are shortages of qualified personnel. And morbidity (of the employee or family members) causes an increase in absenteeism. As a result, service delivery deteriorates and the workload of the employees who are left within the organisation increases.

Although there is evidence that HIV/AIDS has an adverse impact on the public sector, it is usually difficult to determine where the routine problems of a malfunctioning public sector end and where the impact of AIDS starts (Badcock-Walters, Whiteside, 2000). However, the epidemic worsens already existing problems and there is no doubt that the government's capacity to deliver is undermined, especially through the depletion of the human resource base.

HIV/AIDS also affects demand for public services, but the impact is to a great extent sector-specific. Nevertheless, the increase in demand for health services is obvious. This can be illustrated with data from Malawi. According to the Ministry of Health (2001), AIDS-related illness accounted for over 70% of all in-patient admissions: in high-prevalence areas and within certain age groups, the number was even higher. And of 1,225 patients between the ages of 30 and 40 who were admitted to a hospital in Blantyre in 1999-2000, 80% were HIV–positive. This group made up 91% of the patients in the medical ward and 56% of those in surgical wards (Lewis et al., 2003).

The problem with service delivery can be further illustrated by looking at selected indicators for health services in various countries with high HIV-prevalence rates. Table 15 shows that health expenditure as a share of GDP varies greatly, from 9.3% in Malawi to 4.3% in Tanzania. Nevertheless, due to low levels of GDP, annual per capita health expenditure was below US$ 20 in several countries, including Malawi, which can be compared to US$ 2,896 in Sweden. It also shows the severe shortage of health care workers. Tanzania, for example, had 2.3 medical doctors and 36.6 nurses per 100,000 inhabitants in 2004, and the situation was similar in several other countries. In Sweden, there were 319 medical doctors and 953 nurses per 100,000 population.

TABLE 15: SELECTED INDICATORS OF THE QUALITY OF HEALTH SERVICES IN COUNTRIES IN SUB-SAHARAN AFRICA HEAVILY AFFECTED BY HIV/AIDS

Countries	Adult (15–49) HIV prevalence rate [a]	Total health expenditure as % of GDP	Total health expenditure in (US$)/capita[b]	Physicians/ 100,000 population	Nurses/ 100,000 population
	2006	2003	2003	2004	2004
Botswana	24.1	5.6	232	28.8	241.1
Lesotho	23.2	5.6	31	5.4	60.1
Malawi	14.1	9.3	13	1.1	25.6
Mozambique	16.1	4.7	12	2.4	20.5
Namibia	19.6	6.4	99	29.5	168
South Africa	18.8	8.4	295	69.2	388.0
Swaziland	33.4	5.8	107	17.6	320.3
Tanzania	6.4	4.3	12	2.3	36.6
Uganda	6.7	7.3	18	4.7	5.4
Zambia	17.0	5.4	21	6.9	113.1
Zimbabwe	20.1	7.9	40	5.7	54.2
Sweden	0.2	8.3	2,896	319	953

Note: Adapted from Arrehag et al. (2006); [a] Source: UNAIDS (2006); [b] Average exchange rate (in US$).

Sources: WHO (2005a; 2005b); Haacker, (2004), Swedish National Board of Health and Welfare.

There are several reasons for the shortage of qualified staff in the health sectors, but in most countries poor retention of existing staff, particularly in the public sector, and insufficient supply of trained workers are the main ones, as aptly described by Martin-Staple (2004) for Malawi. Migration of health workers has increased during recent years and it is one of the reasons for the problem, as described below.

The private sector is also exposed to HIV/AIDS in various ways. The most immediate impact is likely to be increased costs of production, but also investment and employment are affected.[11] The size of the costs varies greatly across industries. In labour-intensive industries such as transport and commercial farming, productivity is reduced when many infected workers are in the later stages of the disease. However, simple calculations reveal that reductions in productivity associated with poor health for unskilled workers are unlikely to be the main problem: even if 15% of the work force is HIV-positive, only 4% to 5% on average will have reduced working capacity due to illness. Since working capacity for physical work is reduced by 10% to 15% during the last couple of years of the disease, the decline in labour productivity is clearly less than 1%. Hence, the overall impact might not even be noticed, particularly if some workers can be replaced.

The major impact of HIV/AIDS is probably due to loss of skilled workers. This is evident from studies of firms. Jones (1996) evaluated the costs of HIV/AIDS on a tea estate in Malawi. His results showed that the greatest impact of HIV/AIDS on costs and profits was the loss of skilled workers. Since tea production is labour-intensive, this shows that firms that rely heavily on skilled workers may be even more vulnerable. Moreover, many other costs due to HIV/AIDS seem to be equally, or more important than the direct effect of morbidity of workers on labour productivity. Some of these are illness and the death of colleagues, increased workloads and potential stigma and discrimination, which can all contribute to undermining the working morale and consequently reduce labour productivity. Moreover, the structure of employee benefit schemes and how easily employees can be replaced are also important (Whiteside and O'Grady, 2002).

When a company recognises the threat posed by HIV to its employees, it may use three basic strategies for mitigating short and long-term consequences: try to prevent new infections, avoid or reduce the costs associated with existing and future infections and/or provide treatment and support for infected employees to extend their productive working lives and thereby delay the costs of infection (Rosen et al., 2000). Companies use all of these strategies, but the third one, providing anti-retroviral therapy, is becoming more and more common. Under the right circumstances, the private sector can contribute significantly in combating the HIV/AIDS epidemic.

---

11. See UN (2004) for a review of the impact of HIV/AIDS on companies.

8. Gender and economic growth

In sub-Saharan Africa, women are disadvantaged in many respects and the situation is worse than in most other parts of the world. This is evident from the low rankings on UNDP's gender-related development index: the best sub-Saharan country is South Africa, which is ranked 120 out of 177 countries, Gabon is 123, while almost all positions between 141 and 177 are occupied by sub-Saharan countries (UNDP, 2005).

Gender inequality is a multifaceted concept that is hard to measure and the UNDP indexes, constructed by combining several indicators, are clearly tentative. A more robust, but partial, measure of gender inequality is differences in schooling. This measure is used in Table 16 to illustrate the development of one important aspect of gender inequality. The table reports female/male ratios of school attendance for the age group 16 to 20 years. The data come from various demographic and health surveys, which are carried out at irregular intervals in a number of developing countries (ORC Macro, 2007). All sub-Saharan countries with at least two surveys and at least one from 2000 or later are included. Moreover, some recent surveys from a selection of other representative developing countries are added. Data on school attendance from surveys are more informative than the more commonly used national enrolment data, since many children enrol but do not necessarily attend school. The age group 16–20 was chosen because gender differences are much larger for secondary school education. For instance, there are 89 girls to 100 boys enrolled in primary school in sub-Saharan Africa, which is lower then any other region, but far higher than for secondary school attendance (DFID, 2007). Moreover, the economic and social benefits of female secondary education have been recognised recently (Klasen, 2007; Rihani, 2006).

The table shows that there has been some improvement, since countries have higher ratios in the more recent surveys. There are some exceptions though, such as Cameroon and Kenya. The countries with the least inequality are Namibia (0.91), Madagascar (0.75) and Burkina Faso (0.72), and the country with the worst inequality is Chad with 0.34 in 2004, although this is a considerable improvement on the 1990s, when the ratio was 0.23. Nevertheless, it is possible that the table gives too positive a picture, since there have not been any surveys recently in countries with conflicts or political instability. Moreover, there are greater gender differences when completion rates for secondary education are used instead (Rihani, 2006)

Table 16 also highlights the difference between sub-Saharan Africa and other developing countries. Bangladesh, Indonesia and Egypt and Jordan are as good as or better than the best sub-Saharan countries, with the exception of Namibia. However, Cambodia has a ratio of 0.40, demonstrating the variation found in Asia. Latin American countries are uniformly better, as indicated by the ratios for Bolivia, Colombia, Nicaragua and Peru, which are all about one.

Reducing gender inequality is a development goal in its own right, but economic research has mostly focused on its role in promoting economic development. There is a great deal of research at the household level indicating that gender relationships matter for economic development (Knowles et al., 2002; Stotsky, 2006). The direct effect of inequality in education is illustrative. It reduces the average amount of human capital in the country, since qualified girls are not given the opportunity to study. It is also an inefficient allocation of resources, since the marginal return on educating boys and girls most likely are different. Moreover,

TABLE 16: SCHOOL ATTENDANCE RATIOS, GIRLS/BOYS AGED 16 TO 20, SELECTED COUNTRIES

Sub-Saharan Countries		
Burkina Faso 1998/99	Burkina Faso 2003	
0.51	0.72	
Cameron 1991	Cameron 1998	Cameron 2004
0.71	0.64	0.67
Chad 1996/97	Chad 2004	
0.23	0.37	
Eritrea 1995	Eritrea 2002	
0.51	0.48	
Ghana 1993	Ghana 1998	Ghana 2003
0.50	0.63	0.69
Guinea 1999	Guinea 2005	
0.35	0.48	
Kenya 1993	Kenya 1998	Kenya 2003
0.68	0.76	0.72
Madagascar 1992	Madagascar 1997	Madagascar 2003/2004
0.81	0.70	0.75
Malawi 1992	Malawi 2000	Malawi 2004
0.46	0.56	0.56
Mozambique 1997	Mozambique 2003	
0.31	0.57	
Namibia 1992	Namibia 2000	
0.82	0.91	
Nigeria 1990	Nigeria 1999 (1)	Nigeria 2003
0.60	0.69	0.64
Rwanda 1992	Rwanda 2000	Rwanda 2005
0.66	0.63	0.78
Senegal 1992/93	Senegal 2005	
0.44	0.68	
Tanzania 1992	Tanzania 1996	Tanzania 2004
0.46	0.57	0.51
Uganda 1995	Uganda 2000/01	
0.37	0.57	
Zambia 1992	Zambia 1996	Zambia 2001/02 (2)
0.50	0.55	0.53

Non-African Countries		
Bangladesh 2004	Cambodia 2000	Indonesia 2002/2003
0.76	0.40	0.91
Egypt 2000	Jordan 1997	Bolivia 2003
0.77	1.05	0.96
Colombia 2005	Nicaragua 2001	Peru 2000
1.00	1.19	0.96

Source: Demographic and Health Surveys, various years (ORC Macro, 2007)

there are many externalities deriving from female education: for instance, child mortality decreases with the mother's level of education, while the nutritional status and school performance increase. And higher female education reduces fertility, which indirectly affects GDP per capita growth in the long run.

There is relatively little research on the macroeconomic consequences of gender inequality. One reason is the measurement problem. Putting numbers on gender-based violence, exclusion of women from certain economic activities, bargaining power within households, etc., is difficult. Moreover, the most commonly used measure of inequality, income, is only available for households (Klasen, 2005). The alternative is to use non-income inequality measures of well-being. Hence, macro studies have primarily focused on education, but there are some that use health indicators and social capital, such as women's political participation.[12]

In spite of the obvious benefits from increased gender equality at the household level, cross-country studies on economic growth provide a somewhat mixed picture. Reviewing empirical evidence from their own studies, Barro and Sala-i-Martin (2004) argue that only male secondary and college schooling have a positive effect on growth, while female primary schooling has no effect and secondary schooling actually reduces it. These results have been challenged, however. It is not clear how to interpret the coefficients, and the results hinge on the inclusion of Latin American countries, which had low growth and relatively little gender inequality (Klasen, 2002).

Several recent studies find a strong gender effect on economic growth. Knowles et al. (2002) show that female education is more important for labour productivity than male education. Klasen (2002) gets similar results: gender inequality has a strong impact on economic growth, particularly in sub-Saharan Africa. It explains as much as 30% of the difference in growth rates between Botswana, with high growth and low educational gaps, and Ghana and Niger, with substantial gender inequalities. Blackden et al. (2007) analyse growth effects of gender inequality using gender gaps in education, but also in formal sector employment and in access to assets and inputs in agricultural production. Although they do not provide numbers for the combined effects of the gender gaps, their results are suggestive of a substantial impact. For example, a comparison between Uganda and East Asia suggests that gender inequality in education and employment accounts for a difference of 0.7% per year in GDP growth. Hence, Blackden et al. (2007) conclude that "gender inequality acts as a significant constraint to growth in sub-Saharan Africa, and that removing gender-based barriers to growth will make a substantial contribution to realizing Africa's economic potential" (p. 665).

Although limited to developed countries due to the paucity of data, Coulombe and Tremblay (2006) is a relevant study. Using time-series data from literacy tests, a much more exact measure of human capital than the school data, they show that female literacy is both

---

12. See Stotsky (2006) for a thorough review of macroeconomic studies.

more significant and has a stronger impact than male literacy. The literacy skills acquired by one additional year of education increases average GDP per capita growth by 9.45% for females and 5.8% for males.

Hence, investment in female education appears to have a high pay-off both in terms of economic growth, as well as in reduced gender inequality. And the pay-off is likely to be especially high in sub-Saharan Africa, possibly due to the large imbalances. The results from macroeconomic studies on other aspects of gender inequality, such as health and social capital, are not as strong but point in the same direction (Stotsky, 2006).

9. Brain drain

There has been a brain drain from sub-Saharan Africa for a long time, and it has increased significantly since the 1970s, both in absolute and relative terms (Docquier, Rapaport, 2006). In 1990, for which there is reliable data, 11.7% of the skilled workers lived outside sub-Saharan Africa, and in 2000 the number had increased to 12.9% (see Table 17). The total migration rate was much lower, 0.7% in 1990 and 0.9% in 2000. The migration of skilled workers varies greatly across regions and countries: in Eastern Africa the migration rate was as high as 18.6% for skilled workers in 2000. In several countries the rates were even higher: as many as 42% of those with tertiary education had migrated from Ghana by 2000, 25.6% from Angola and 26.3% from Kenya. The migration rate for Sweden, for example, was 4.4% (see Docquier and Marfouk, 2006).

Another way of looking at migration is to compare the share of skilled workers among the residents in the home country and the migrants. In EU15, 18.6% of the residents are skilled and 32.6% are skilled among those that migrate from EU15. The corresponding numbers for sub-Saharan Africa are 2.8% and 42.5% (Docquier, 2007).

TABLE 17: MIGRATION RATES IN 1990 AND 2000 (IN %)

Region	Migration rate in 1990		Migration rate in 2000	
	Total	Skilled	Total	Skilled
Sub-Saharan countries	0.7	11.7	0.9	12.9
Eastern Africa	0.8	15.4	1.0	18.6
Middle Africa	0.8	12.1	1.0	16.1
Southern Africa	0.6	9.1	1.0	6.8
Western Africa	0.6	10.4	1.0	14.8
Northern Europe	6.6	14.0	6.8	13.7

Note: The migration rate is defined as the stock of migrants abroad (outside the region indicated) as a percentage of those at home.
Source: Docquier and Rapoport (2006).

Generally, brain drain is considered to be unfavourable for the migrants' home country and favourable to the recipient. This is because governments invest in education and training but receive little in return when skilled people migrate. However, brain drain does not have only negative effects on those left behind. Migration of skilled workers generates remittances; it improves business and trade networks; increases expected returns to education; and leads to increased knowledge and skills when migrants return home (Docquier, 2007; Kuznetsov, Sabel, 2006). It is, for example, easy to appreciate the importance of remittances: over the period 2000–05, official remittances to sub-Saharan Africa were 2.5% of GDP, but some countries received well over 5%, such as Lesotho, Cape Verde, Guinea-Bissau and Senegal (Gupta et al., 2007). Moreover, unrecorded remittances might be as high as 50% of the recorded ones (Freund, Spatafora, 2005). A large part of these are likely to be due to the migration of skilled workers.

Studies of the costs and benefits of migration have been fraught with data problems, but recently new much improved data have been compiled. Docquier and Rapoport (2006) use these to analyse migration from the perspective of developing countries and conclude that optimal skilled migration is positive: this means there should be some net skilled migration from poor countries. Beine et al. (2007) also evaluate the net effect of the brain drain, but over a large cross-section of countries. They find that migration increases the number of skilled workers living in developing countries: the brain drain thus has a positive effect in the aggregate. However, there are distributional consequences. Among countries with low levels of human capital, those with a large share of unskilled migration tend to gain, while those with large shares of skilled migrants lose. Small countries in sub-Saharan Africa and Central America clearly have too much migration of skilled workers.

A case where the brain drain is very likely to have a negative impact is migration of health workers from countries with high HIV rates. The lack of medical doctors and nurses is evident from Table 15 above. Unfortunately, HIV/AIDS seems to worsen the problem. Bhargava and Docquier (2007) combine cross-country data on brain drain with UNAIDS prevalence rates for countries in sub-Saharan Africa and find a positive relationship between HIV/AIDS prevalence and the migration of physicians. Hence, HIV/AIDS seems to cause migration.

The problem is also illustrated by Figure 3, which depicts migration rates for physicians from 1991 to 2004 for selected countries in sub-Saharan Africa. The migration rate is defined as the stock of physicians abroad as a per cent of physicians trained in the country. As the graph shows, in most countries over 10% of the medical doctors worked abroad, and in Malawi and Zimbabwe the rates were over 25% during 2000–04. Hence, there is an urgent need for action, both for sub-Saharan countries losing skilled workers and for the recipient countries, as well for donors and international organisations. A recent initiative by DFID in Malawi to top up salaries for health workers and provide incentives to attract Malawian doctors and nurses working abroad to return home, is one interesting attempt to alleviate problems caused by the brain drain (see Palmer, 2006).

FIGURE 3: MIGRATION RATES FOR PHYSICIANS IN SELECTED SUB-SAHARAN COUNTRIES, 1991–2004

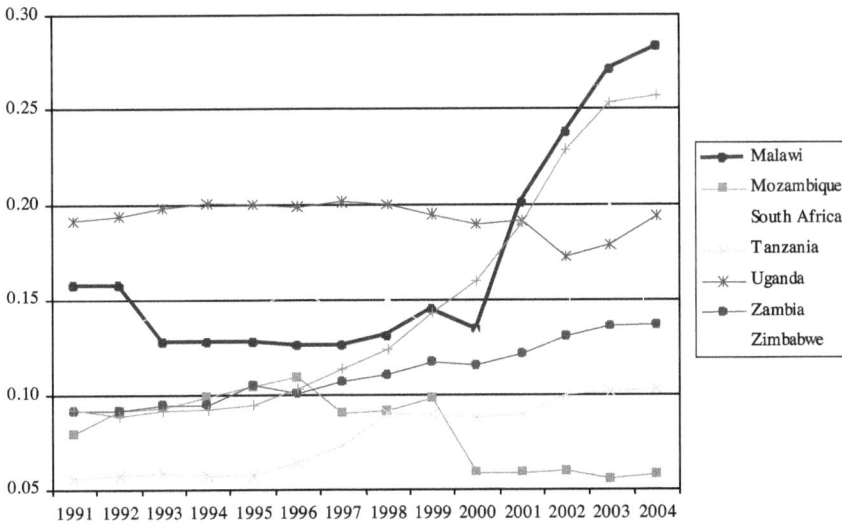

Source: Adapted from Arrehag et al. (2008). The data are from Bhargava and Docquier, (2006).

49

10. Trade policy reform and African development [13]

There is an extensive literature on the trade-growth relationship. This is a somewhat contro-versial literature since it is hard to show a clear casual relationship,[14] but it is abundantly clear the countries that have succeeded in increasing income levels substantially have also been successful in the export markets. The gains are partly static gains of specialisation and partly due to dynamic gains in the form of positive effects on total factor productivity (see Bigsten et al., 2004, for evidence on productivity effects of exports in African manufacturing).

Trade policy vis-á-vis Africa is thus important. Estimates using the linkage model of the global economy (Anderson, Martin, van der Mensbrugghe, 2006; World Bank, 2006) suggest that full liberalisation of global merchandise trade would increase world GDP by US$ 287 bn per year by 2015 and, of this, US$ 86 bn would accrue to the developing countries.[15] These estimates disregard gains from service trade liberalisation, trade facilitation and productivity gains from opening up. Sub-Saharan Africa would experience an income increase of US$ 4.8 bn or 1.1% of its GDP, which seems modest but still represents a relative income gain for the region that is double the world average. Two-thirds of the gains are due to reforms in other countries and a third is due to own reforms. In the case of complete global trade liber-alisation, as much as 78% of the gains for sub-Saharan Africa would come from agricultural reforms in all countries (textile and clothing contributes 11%, other merchandise 11%), and essentially the whole gain to Africa from EU liberalisation would come from the elimination of its various agricultural protection measures. These reforms would also have a positive distributional impact in the developing countries, since it is farmers and unskilled labour that are most likely to gain from the trade liberalisation (Hertel, Winters, 2006).

However, full liberalisation of merchandise trade is not likely in the short term. What has been attempted during the last five years is a multilateral agreement within the WTO frame-work. The aim of the Doha Round was to achieve multilateral, reciprocal, non-discriminato-ry trade liberalisation. A successful completion of the round would have implied significantly lower levels of protection, although still some way from full free trade. Anderson, Martin and van der Mensbrugghe (2006) simulate various possible outcomes of the negotiations and find that the effect on global real income by 2015 would be in the range of US$ 75–120 bn. In these scenarios, however, almost all of the gains accrue to the reforming high-income countries, while the impact on sub-Saharan Africa specifically would be modest. Thus, the 'concessions' that the EU and other industrialised countries are willing to make would largely benefit themselves. For the Doha Round to benefit Africa, much more is needed. It would be important to transfer some of the gains from the liberalisation from the EU[16] to Africa in the form of more aid, for example, to develop supply capacities in sub-Saharan Africa via improvements in transport and market infrastructure, training and extension (see Hertel and Winters, 2006).

To be able to integrate with the world economy, African countries need to have an eco-nomic environment that makes it possible for them to be an arena for outsourcing and FDI generally. This requires systems that can guarantee quality and timely deliveries. If products

---

13. This section draws on Bigsten (2007).
14. See, for example the critical review of the evidence by Rodriguez and Rodrik (2001)
15. Cline (2004) found that the impact of a complete removal of tariffs on developing countries would be a long-run income gain of about US$ 200 bn per year and that about half of this would be due to removal by developed countries of import tariffs against developing countries. He also found that the impact on poverty would be large.
16. EU25+EFTA would gain US$ 65 bn according to these model simulations.

are part of production process or a marketing drive, it is fatal to deliver late. Stability and security is therefore essential for LDCs if they are to be able to benefit from the forces of globalisation. The World Bank (2006, p. 94) notes that a typical import transaction in Africa takes 58 days versus 14 days in industrialised countries and that each day of delay reduces exports by 1%.

African countries are at present covered by the EU General System of Preferences, but this does not seem to have had a large effect on African exports. The fact that other parts of the world have done much better in terms of export expansion suggests that African countries suffer from major supply side constraints. In the last couple of years, the resource boom in oil and other natural resources has increased export incomes and sub-Saharan Africa saw incomes from merchandise exports increase by 27% in 2005 (World Bank, 2006, p 114). So there have been some improvements in recent years because of the boom, but how long this will last is an open question.

Sub-Saharan African countries not only face high tariffs in the developed countries, but even higher tariffs on their trade with other developing countries (World Bank, 2005). Even if countries in sub-Saharan Africa face low tariffs in manufacturing, they face high restrictions on their most important exports, agriculture.

Agriculture is in focus in the Doha Round, but this is a politically sensitive sector although it is no longer very important economically in the richer regions. The protectionist measures applied within the EU reduce the welfare of EU citizens while at the same time holding down incomes in Africa. It should be easy to get an agreement between the parties, but the agricultural lobbies in the North are very strong.

There is a system of trade preferences in place, which matters for poor African economies. In 2005, the EC introduced a more generous system of preferences that offers duty-free access for 80% of the dutiable tariff lines to a set of poor countries that meet certain criteria. However, the existing system of trade preferences for the ACP countries is against WTO rules. They discriminate against developing countries that are not in the ACP group, and they lack reciprocity, which is another requirement. The EU and the ACP countries did not manage to finalise a new arrangement during the Cotonou negotiation, so the WTO granted them an 8-year waiver that expires at the end of 2007. The EPAs covering trade relations and EU assistance measures plus measures to enhance intra-regional and international integration therefore need to be put in place shortly (unless another extension can be obtained). Negotiations are continuing, but so far progress has been slow.

EU tariffs on, for example, agricultural goods remain and they are very detrimental to African countries. There is also a need for reforms in other areas, such as rules of origin, technical standards, quotas and subsidies. The African and other ACP countries should be allowed to reduce their tariffs on EU exports at a slower pace. Such an asymmetrical timetable would be acceptable to the WTO, but would have to end within a reasonable period. Milner, Morrissey and McKay (2005) suggest that ten years would be a reasonable estimate of that time, which means that markets would be open by 2018. Eventually the services trade should also be included in these arrangements. Systems of regulation should also be improved to facilitate investment and institutions that facilitate trade need to be developed.

Simulations of the effects of EPAs (e.g., Milner, Morrissey, McKay, 2005) find that the short-run welfare effects will be limited, and it is also shown that African economies would have relatively more to gain from unilateral liberalisation as against all countries, not EU only.

Such measures would be more growth-enhancing since they would be less discriminatory. Particularly the LDCs have relatively little to gain with regard to trade from entering into EPAs, since they already have almost free access to the EU market under the 'Everything But Arms' initiative. They will get even better access in the future as the remaining tariffs and quotas on bananas, rice and sugar will be phased out by July 2009. The LDCs will then have full and free market access to the EU market (including the commodities currently subject to the EU's commodity protocols with the ACP countries). However, these countries still face the risk that the EU may use various safeguard clauses to stem export surges and countries may be eliminated from the generous treatment when they graduate from the LDC category.

It may be hard to entice the LDCs to enter into EPAs unless some further benefits are offered. Such measures could include simpler and less restrictive rules of origin, concessions on trade in services, reduction in non-tariff barriers, financial support to help the LDCs deal with the adjustment costs and technical assistance to help them develop their exports (Borrmann, Busse, Neuhas, 2004). The members not in the least developed category will see larger benefits from entering into the EPAs, since they do not have the same advantages at present. EPAs would also be more beneficial than the more restrictive Generalised System of Preferences option.

The EPAs will lead to a reduction in tariff revenues, which is often a substantial share of government revenue in sub-Saharan Africa. This is a concern if the expected expansion of export incomes is slow in coming, which would be the case in the least efficient economies. They need to replace the foregone tariff revenues with other government incomes, avoid substantial trade diversion, regulate liberalised services industries and manage intra-regional trade more effectively (Hinkle, Schiff, 2004).

In spite of the adjustment problems, the EPA process may have beneficial long-term effects. It needs to be supported by other measures to facilitate export expansion in ACP countries. One should utilise the EPAs as instruments of development (Hinkle, Schiff, 2004). EPAs should be followed by measures in other areas such as exchange rate policy, trade facilitation measures, investment climate, and competition policy and infrastructure investment. Multilateral liberalisation might be superior, but even if the countries go for that they could still have EPAs as well to get some of the non-trade benefits associated with them (Gasiorek, Winter, 2004).[17]

Countries that do not enter into EPAs will be left with the GSP, but they may lose the extra aid disbursements and technical assistance in association with the EPAs. They will face a considerable erosion of the margin of preferences they will receive on the export to the EU. Regional integration may help to increase export supply, but the major challenge is to improve domestic policies and institutions.

---

17. When it comes to the liberalisation of services, Jansen (2006) concludes that in general the multilateral route seems preferable. Why allow only EU firms entry, if there are better alternatives available elsewhere?

11. The role of principal internal and external economic actors

The role of different actors in the African economy has been discussed throughout this report, but in this section we add some comments on the main internal and external actors in the economic sphere and discuss their roles in the economic development of Africa.

For Africa to take off economically, economic agents there have to be put in a context where they have incentives and opportunities to invest and to allocate resources efficiently. The economic agents we are talking of here are households, firms and farms. The economic environment in Africa has not been so benevolent, but it has been improved in many countries over the most recent decade. Still, it remains true that the economic environment in Africa is more risky than that in other regions for several reasons. There are, for example, climate risks that make it hard to be a farmer in Africa. There are also economic risks associated with the specialisation of African economies on certain natural resources or crops, for which prices on the world market may fluctuate. There are policy risks, in the sense that the political environment is often unstable, and this makes it hard to make long-term investment decisions. In recent years, political conflicts have in several instances escalated into full-blown civil wars, sometimes with neighbouring countries being drawn into them.

Thus, Africa is a region with unusually high economic risks. This means that investors, domestic as well as international, demand a very high risk premium on their investments a. This holds back African investments. The fact that economic returns on investments in Africa are high, which has been enthusiastically reported in the press, is therefore not necessarily a positive signal. High returns indicate that only the few investments that have high returns occur, while projects with returns that would have sufficed in other regions never take place. The high rates of return have obviously not been high enough to attract large investment resources into Africa. It was even estimated a few years ago that Africans themselves held 40% of their capital outside Africa (Collier, Hoeffler, Pattillo, 2001).

The quality and stability of the economic environment within which economic agents operate depends on the institutional structure, and the quality of the government is of course central here. We have argued that the poor institutional and policy quality is the most important constraint on African growth. There has in recent years been a process of democratisation and some improvement in the functioning of governments, but the low quality of governance is still the most severe development problem in Africa. There is by now a reasonable consensus among economic analysts with regard to what needs to be done, but it is not clear how one can make governments want to do the right thing and manage to do so. It is at the same time an incentive, competence and resource issue.

The question then is how such incentives for governments can be provided. The normal procedure in a democracy is of course that the government is under the control of the electorate with the help of the media and various civil society organisations. During the period of structural adjustment, democracy in Africa was poor and the donors sought to come up with an alternative control mechanism. The approach chosen was to use policy conditionalities in connection with the resource transfers to force governments to pursue 'sensible' policies. These policies were mostly reasonable, and many governments also said they agreed and would pursue them. However, often they chose to back-track once they had received the loan, or the implementation was haphazard since the government did not feel it was its own policy. The poor efficiency of this approach led to increasing scepticism about conditionality, and the debate on ownership followed. This led to reform of the system of conditionalities with more emphasis on control by the recipient government of policy-formulation, but with more extensive exchanges of views with various strata of the society, including donors. This has led to some reduction in policy conditionalities, but is not really a radical departure. It may be noted that international economic integration can help restrain government, since the costs of economically irresponsible policy changes become quickly apparent (Bigsten, Durevall, 2003).

12. Concluding remarks

African economies had stagnating or falling per capita incomes from the early 1970s to the mid-1990s. Then a modest reversal started and during the last few years per capita incomes have been growing at a decent 3% per year. If this rate can be sustained until 2015 and in-equality does not increase, Africa has a chance of reaching the MDG for poverty reduction (Bigsten and Shimeles, 2007).[18] The growth acceleration is partly due to the ongoing resource boom, but improvements in economic policies have also contributed. Policies need to be improved further, but the greatest political challenge is now in respect of implementation, where the severe problems are due both to lack of competence and lack of incentives to do the right things.

Africa is the poorest region in the world and its social problems are huge. It is also the region that has been worst hit by the HIV/AIDS epidemic. Although it is difficult to de-termine the epidemic's detrimental effects with any precision, a vast number of empirical studies indicate that they are substantial. It is also clear that HIV/AIDS is a major obstacle to reaching several of the MDGs in the worst affected countries. On a more positive note, the distribution of anti-retroviral therapy is being scaled-up rapidly in many countries and there are signs of declining prevalence in some of them, particularly in large cities. Moreover, more governments take the threat of HIV/AIDS seriously. If policy efforts are sustained, they can make a difference, as is evident from the experiences of Senegal and Uganda.

There are numerous studies that show the negative effects of gender inequality at the household level, but it has been more difficult to identify an impact on income at a national level. One reason is probably measurement problems. Many aspects of gender inequality are simply not quantifiable. However, recent studies, using schooling data, have found strong effects in sub-Saharan Africa.

The brain drain from Africa has increased since the early 1990s, and is seemingly still growing. Recent research has shown that it is not necessarily bad that skilled workers mi-grate from a poor country. Migration of skilled workers generates remittances, it improves business and trade networks, increases expected returns to education, and leads to increased knowledge and skills when migrants return home. Nevertheless, for most sub-Saharan na-tions, skilled migration is too high. There is thus a need for policies that make it less attractive to migrate and encourage skilled workers return.

To be able to reduce poverty and to deal with social problems, African economies need sustained growth. The economic prospects for African economies depend on whether they can make a breakthrough in the export markets. This will in turn depend on the trade policies pursued by the EU, in addition to those of China and India. Sweden has long had a liberal stand on trade reform and should try to convince other EU members that Europe needs to pursue free trade strategies. The Common Agricultural Policy is a disgrace that makes both African and European consumers poorer.

For Africa to sustain the growth process and to achieve a real economic take-off, it must become an attractive arena for private sector investment, and for that to happen it must

---

18. The results of simulations between 2001 and 2015 based on the World Development Indicator (2004) distribution data indicate that the average growth rate in per capita consumption required to meet MDG1 with a neutral pattern of growth is around 2.1%, while the median is slightly lower (1.9%), with notable variation across countries, from a high of 4.9% for Central African Republic to a low of 0.7% for Morocco and South Africa. Considering a long-term average population growth rate of around 2.4% (WDI, 2006), the growth in consumption expenditure needed is about 4.5%. The results indicate that by holding inequality at its current level, most African countries would be able to achieve MDG1 with relatively modest (but sustained) growth rates.

provide an economic environment that is conducive to export production. Unless investors, domestic or foreign, find it in their interest to use Africa as a base for production for the world market, the investment boom will not happen.

China's and India's trade and investments in sub-Saharan Africa have risen dramatically during recent years, creating a further opportunity for the integration of Africa into the global economy. The final impact will to a large extent be determined by policies adopted in sub-Saharan Africa to improve the functioning of markets, but also to some extent by China and India, which still have tariffs on some agricultural commodities. Donors and international organisations also have an important role to play, providing technical assistance to strengthen trade-related institutions and improve policy implementation.

Aid and debt relief should contribute to the creation of an environment where private investments can succeed, and thereby achieve long-term poverty reduction. So far aid has made a positive contribution to African economic growth, even if the overall impact has been less than hoped for. However, in many countries the economic situation is more promising than it has been for a long time, and the chances of positive impacts from aid interventions are higher than earlier.

The chances are good that aid will increase in the future, and more aid has been pledged by donors. At the Millennium Summit of 2000, world leaders agreed on a set of common development targets, the Millennium Development Goals, for development efforts until 2015. In 2005, proposals for massive increases in aid to particularly Africa were presented by the UN (2005) and the Commission for Africa (2005). In terms of the promises made by Western countries, for example at the G8 meeting at Gleneagles in 2005, the aid flow to Africa should increase rapidly over the next few years. There is also agreement within the EU that all (the old) members will give at least 0.56% of GNI as aid by 2010 and 0.7% by 2015. Sweden of course already surpasses this figure, while the average for the whole of (old) EU was 0.35% in 2004 (Bigsten, 2007). Whether the member countries will live up to these promises remains to be seen.

The impact of increased aid flows will depend on the modalities for its transfer. Collier (2006) argues for governance conditionality aimed at weakening the dominance of the governing elite. Democracy has two important dimensions, electoral competition and checks and balances. Countries need system scrutiny to achieve honesty and other systems to achieve efficiency. Since scrutiny is a public good, it is subject to collective action problems, and donors could here help organise citizens. They could also stimulate peer group evaluations. Donors could help improve information to the citizens, build up their capacity to analyse it and promote incentives for agents to perform. Once a system is there, donors have an important role to play by insisting that rewards and penalties are built in and are implemented. Audit systems and parliamentary scrutiny are key areas of intervention. Thus, a crucial aim of donors should be to improve governance and implementation capacity in recipient countries. This requires a shift towards governance conditionality combined with technical assistance to build up systems that can handle government resources in a transparent and accountable way.

For this to work, there is need for donor coordination (Bigsten, 2006). UNDP has never managed to bring this about although it was its original mandate, but the World Bank and the IMF have had such a role. A possible coordinator in the case of European aid would be the EU, but so far it has not performed this task. EU aid has been quite bureaucratic and inefficient, although there have been some improvements in recent years (Berlin, Resare,

2005). By shifting aid towards more general forms of aid such as budget support, donors may reduce the coordination problem and possibly also increase ownership. When different donors finance the same project or programmes, they could appoint one of their number to be the coordinating agent responsible for government contacts and follow up.

The EU and the whole of the OECD have often reiterated the need for policy coherence for development (OECD, 2003). Sweden has adopted an official policy that tries to ensure that all policies are consistent with the aim of global development and poverty reduction in poor countries (Sweden, 2001). The EU has similar ambitions (OECD, 2002, p. 43). Policies across various ministries as well as across various countries should thus support the overall goal of development in LDCs and create synergies among themselves. The action on coherence among decision makers is limited and there is a lack of capacity to monitor policy coherence. It may be overambitious to take the development impact of all policies into account, but EU members should at least try to improve the coherence of the policies that are most important to LDCs. The most problematic political areas for policy change of the sort discussed in this paper are not aid policy but trade policy and the CAP. This is a challenge to EU policy makers, since changes to the latter areas are probably the most important if we are serious about our commitment to development.

Appendix: Data

The table shows aggregate net resource flows, which is the divided into official resource flows (aid) and private flows. In the latter category we have the important foreign direct investment category, which is also reported separately.

APPENDIX TABLE 1: CAPITAL FLOWS TO MAJOR REGIONS 1970–2005 (IN BILLION CURRENT US DOLLARS)

		1970	1975	1980	1985	1990	1995	2000	2005
East Asia & Pacific	Aggregate net resource flows (US$)	1.95	6.54	9.15	12.51	25.09	84.54	46.52	133.35
	Official net resource flows (US$)	1.09	1.85	3.52	4.54	7.92	12.39	7.86	3.17
	Private net resource flows (US$)	0.86	4.69	5.64	7.96	17.16	72.15	38.66	130.18
	Foreign direct investment, net inflows (US$)	0.42	1.87	1.50	2.95	10.51	50.80	45.14	96.90
Europe & Central Asia	Aggregate net resource flows (US$)	0.48	0.70	6.32	5.29	8.20	31.11	48.75	161.52
	Official net resource flows (US$)	0.34	0.54	3.61	2.31	4.24	10.80	9.33	-22.40
	Private net resource flows (US$)	0.13	0.16	2.71	2.98	3.97	20.31	39.42	183.92
	Foreign direct investment, net inflows (US$)	0.15	0.17	0.71	1.03	3.33	14.80	25.37	73.69
Latin America & Caribbean	Aggregate net resource flows (US$)	4.54	15.32	29.58	15.85	22.25	72.55	89.53	100.12
	Official net resource flows (US$)	0.96	2.85	4.72	7.17	9.01	12.38	2.08	1.19
	Private net resource flows (US$)	3.57	12.47	24.86	8.68	13.24	60.17	87.45	98.93
	Foreign direct investment, net inflows (US$)	1.40	3.24	6.36	5.97	8.24	30.51	80.02	70.02
Middle East & North Africa	Aggregate net resource flows (US$)	1.01	8.72	12.69	11.04	9.88	3.16	6.41	21.73
	Official net resource flows (US$)	0.57	5.58	9.22	7.51	9.56	0.98	0.55	0.73
	Private net resource flows (US$)	0.44	3.14	3.47	3.53	0.32	2.18	5.86	21.01
	Foreign direct investment, net inflows (US$)	0.16	0.81	1.46	1.50	0.74	0.95	4.83	13.77
South Asia	Aggregate net resource flows (US$)	1.36	3.74	6.28	7.07	8.99	9.13	13.54	31.69
	Official net resource flows (US$)	1.27	3.65	5.04	4.65	6.86	2.96	2.88	8.40
	Private net resource flows (US$)	0.09	0.09	1.24	2.42	2.14	6.16	10.66	23.29
	Foreign direct investment, net inflows (US$)	0.07	0.01	0.19	0.26	0.54	2.93	4.36	9.87
Sub-Saharan Africa	Aggregate net resource flows (US$)	2.08	5.38	11.53	8.88	18.58	22.77	21.95	56.84
	Official net resource flows (US$)	0.89	3.38	7.18	8.90	16.53	14.23	10.68	30.45
	Private net resource flows (US$)	1.19	2.00	4.35	-0.22	2.05	8.54	11.27	26.39
	Foreign direct investment, net inflows (US$)	0.83	0.81	0.19	0.91	1.21	4.52	6.80	16.56

Source. GDF 2007

References

Acemoglu, D., Johnson, S., Robinson, J.A. (2001), "The Colonial Origins of Comparative Development: An Empirical Investigation", *American Economic Review* 91(5):1369–1401.

Acemoglu, D., Johnson, S., Robinson, J.A. (2002), "Reversal of Fortune: Geography and Institutions in the Making of the Modern World Income Distribution", *Quarterly Journal of Economics* 117(4):1231–94.

Acemoglu, D., Johnson, S., Robinson, J.A. (2003), "An African Success Story: Botswana". In D. Rodrik (ed.), *In search of prosperity: analytic narratives on economic growth*. Princeton: Princeton University Press.

Addison, T. (2006), "Debt Relief", *Swedish Economic Policy Review* 16(2).

Anderson, K., Martin, W., van der Mensbrugghe, D. (2006), Doha Merchandise Trade Reform: What's at stake for Developing Countries? Policy Research Working Paper 3848, World Bank, Washington DC.

Arndt, C., Lewis, J. (2001), "The HIV/AIDS pandemic in South Africa: sectoral impacts and unemployment", *Journal of International Development* 13:427–49

Arrehag, L., de Vylder, S, Durevall, D. Sjöblom, M. (2006), *The impact of HIV/AIDS on Livelihoods, Poverty and the Economy of Malawi,* Sida Studies no. 18.

Artadi, E., Sala-i-Martin, X. (2003), "The Economic Tragedy of the XXth Century: Growth in Africa". NBER Working Paper no. 9865. Cambridge MA.

Badcock-Walters, P. and Whiteside, A. (2000), "HIV/AIDS and Development in the Education Sector", Health Economics & HIV/AIDS Research Division (HEARD), University of KwaZulu-Natal, Durban.

Barrro, R., Sala-i-Marin, X. (2004), *Economic Growth*. Cambridge MA: MIT Press.

Barnett, T., Whiteside, A. (2002), *AIDS in the Twenty-First Century: Disease and Globalization*. Basingstoke: Palgrave-Macmillan.

Beegle, K., De Weerdt, J., Dercon, S. (2006), "Orphanhood and the Long-run Impact on Children", *American Journal of Agricultural Economics* 88():1266–77.

Beegle, K., De Weerdt, J., Dercon, S. (2007), "Adult Mortality and Economic Growth in the Age of HIV/AIDS", *Economic Development and Cultural Change*, forthcoming.

Beine, M., Docquier, F., Rapoport, H. (2007), "Brain drain and human capital formation in developing countries: winners and losers", *Economic Journal*, forthcoming.

Bell, C. Devarajan, S., Gersbach, H. (2004), "Thinking About the Long-Run Economic Costs of AIDS". In Haacker, M. (ed.), *The Macroeconomics of HIV/AIDS*. Washington DC: IMF.

Bennell P. (2005) "The impact of the AIDS Epidemic on Teachers in Sub-Saharan Africa", *Journal of Development Studies* 41(3).

Berlin, A., Resare, N. (2005), *The European Community's External Actions. A Development Perspective*. Stockholm: Sida.

Bhargava, A. and F. Docquier (2006), "HIV Prevalence, Migration of Health Care Staff and Economic Activity in Africa". Mimeo. Washington DC: World Bank.

Bigsten, A. (2006), "Coordination et utilisations des aides", *Revue d'Economie du Developpement* 2:77–103.

Bigsten, A. (2007), "EU Development Policy: The Way Forward". In Sapir, A. (ed.), *The Fragmented Power*. Brussels: Bruegel.

Bigsten, A., Collier, P., Dercon, S., Fafchamps, M., Gauthier, B., Gunning, J.W., Oduro, A., Oostendorp, R., Pattillo, C., Söderbom, M., Teal, F., Zeufack, A. (2004), "Do African Firms Learn from Exporting?", *Journal of Development Studies* 40(3):115–71.

Bigsten, A., Durevall, D. (2003), "Globalisation and Policy Effects in Africa", *The World Economy* 26(8):1119–36.

Bigsten, A., Shimeles, S. (2007), "Can Africa Reduce Poverty by Half by 2015?", (with Abebe Shimeles), *Development Policy Review* 25(2):147–66.

Bigsten, A., Söderbom, M. (2006), "What Have We Learned from a Decade of Manufacturing Enterprise Surveys in Africa?", *World Bank Research Observer* 21(2):241–65

Bigsten, A., Söderbom, M. (2007), "Vad krävs för att tillverkningsindustrin i Afrika ska växa?", *Ekonomisk debatt*, forthcoming.

Birdsall, N., Hamoudi, A. (2004), "AIDS and the Accumulation and Utilization of Human Capital in Africa". In Haacker, M. (ed.), *The Macroeconomics of HIV/AIDS*. Washington DC: IMF.

Blackden, Mark, Sudarshan Canagarajah, David Lawson (2007), "Gender and Growth in Sub-Saharan Africa: Evidence and Issues". In Mavrotas, G. and A. Shorrocks (eds.), *Advancing Development*. London: Palgrave, pp. 349–370.

Bloom, D., Mahal, A. (2007), "Does the AIDS Epidemic threaten Economic Growth", *Journal of Econometrics* 77:105–24.

Bollinger, L., Stover, J., Enock Palamuleni, M. (2000), "The Economic Impact of AIDS in Malawi". Mimeo, The Futures Group International, POLICY Project. Washington, DC.

Bonnel, R. (2000), "HIV/AIDS and Economic Growth: a Global Perspective", *Journal of South African Economics* 68(5):820–55.

Borrmann, A., Busse, M., Neuhaus, S. (2005), "EU/ACP Economic Partnership Agreements: Impact, Options and Prerequisites", *Intereconomics* 40(3):169–76.

Broadman, H.G. (2007), *Africa's Silk Road: China and India's New Economic Frontier*. Washington DC: World Bank.

Burnside, C., Dollar, D. (2000), "Aid, policies, and growth", *American Economic Review* 90:847–68.

Business Report (2007), "China's Africa trade shoots up by 40%", May 14, 2007. Avalaible on line http://www.busrep.co.za/index.php?fSectionId=565&fArticleId=3829372

Casale, M. (2005), "The Impact of HIV/AIDS on Poverty, Inequality and Economic Growth". Mimeo, HEARD, University of Kwazulu-Natal, Durban.

Clemens, M.A., Radelet, S., Bhavnani, R. (2004), Counting Chickens when they hatch: the short-term effect of aid on growth", Center for Global Development, Washington DC.

Cline W.R. (2004), *Trade Policy and Global Poverty*, Center for Global Development and Institute for International Economics, Washington DC

Collier, P. (2006), "Africa: An Agenda for Decisive Change", *Swedish Economic Policy Review* 16(2).

Collier, P. (2007), Post-Conflict Recovery: How Should Policies be Distinctive? Paper presented at the AERC Biannual workshop, Nairobi, mimeo.

Collier, P., Hoeffler, A. (2004), "Greed and Grievance in Civil War", *Oxford Economic Papers* 56(4):563–95.

Collier, P., O'Connell, S. (2004), "Opportunities, Syndromes and Episodes". Draft of chapter 2 in *Explaining African Economic Growth*, Cambridge University Press, forthcoming.

Collier, P., Hoeffler A., Pattillo, C. (2001), "Flight Capital as a Portfolio Choice", *The World Bank Economic Review* 15:55–80.

Coulombe, S., Tremblay, J-F. (2006), "Literacy and Growth", *Topics in Macroeconomics* 6(2):1–32.

Commission for Africa (2005), *Our Common Interest: Report of the Commission for Africa*. London.

Corrigan, P., Glomm, G., Mendez, F. (2005), "AIDS Crisis and Growth", *Journal of Development Economics* 77(1):107–24.

Crafts, N., Venables, A. (2002), "Globalization in History: A Geographical Perspective". Discussion Paper 3079. Centre for Economic Policy Research, London School of Economics.

Cuddington, J., Hancock, J. (1994), "Assessing the Impact of AIDS on the Growth Path of the Malawian Economy", *Journal of Development Economics* 43.

De Waal, (2006), AIDS and power: Why there is no political crisis – yet. New York: Zed Books.

DFID (2007) "Girls Education", *Factsheet* January 2007.

Docquier, F. (2007), "Brain drain and inequality across nations", *Revue d'Economie du Développement,* reprinted in the Proceedings of the 4the AFD/EUDN conference, forthcoming.

Docquier, F., Marfouk, A. (2006), "International migration by educational attainment (1990–2000) – Release 1.1". In C. Ozden and M. Schiff (eds), *International Migration, Remittances and Development.* New York: Palgrave-Macmillan.

Docquier, F., Rapoport, H. (2006), "Skilled migration: The perspective of developing countries". In J. Baghwati and G. Hanson (eds), *Skilled migration: prospects, problems and policies.* New York: Russell Sage Foundation (2006), forthcoming.

Dollar, D., Easterly, W. (1999), "The Search for the Key: Aid, Investment, and Policies in Africa". Policy Research Working Paper no 2070. Washington DC: World Bank.

Doucouliagos, H., Paldam, M. (2006), "Aid Effectiveness on Accumulation: a Meta-Study", *Kyklos* 59:227–54.

Easterly, W. (2001), "The Lost Decades: Developing Countries' Stagnation in Spite of Policy Reform 1980–1998", *Journal of Economic Growth* 6(2):135–57.

Fortson, J. (2006), "Mortality Risk and Human Capital Investment: The Impact of HIV/AIDS in Sub-Saharan Africa". Mimeo, Deptartment of Economics, Princeton University.

Freund, C., Spatafora, N. (2005), "Remittances: Transaction Costs, Determinants, and Informal Flows". World Bank Policy Research Paper No. 3704, Washington, DC.

Gasiorek, M., Winters, L.A. (2004), "What Role for the EPAs in the Caribbean?", *World Economy* 27(9):1335–62.

Gupta, S., Pattillo, C., Wagh, S. (2007), "Impact of Remittances on Poverty and Financial Development in Sub-Saharan Africa". IMF Working Paper 07/38, Washington DC.

Haacker, M. (2002), "The Economic Consequences of HIV/AIDS in Southern Africa". Working paper WP/02/38, IMF, Washington DC.

Haacker, M.(ed.), (2004), *The Macroeconomics of HIV/AIDS.* Washington; IMF.

Hall, R.E., Jones, C.I. (1999), "Why Do Some Countries Produce so Much More Output per Worker than others", *Quarterly Journal of Economics* 114(1):83–116.

Hammarskjöld, M. (2004), "HIV/AIDS – Is the Worst Yet to Come? Data, Spread pattern and Trends". Chapter 9 in *One Step Further: Responses to HIV/AIDS,* Sida Studies no.7, Stockholm.

Hamoudi, A. Birdsall, N. (2004), "AIDS and the accumulation and utilisation of human capital in Africa", *Journal of African Economies* 13(suppl 1).

Hausmann, R., Pritchett, L., Rodrik, D. (2004), "Growth Accelerations". NBER Working Paper No. 10566, Cambridge MA.

Hertel, T.W., Winters, L.A. (eds) (2006), *Poverty and the WTO: Impacts of the Doha Development Agenda.* New York: Palgrave-Macmillan.

Hinkle, L.E., Schiff, M. (2004), "Economic Partnership Agreements between Sub-Saharan Africa and the EU: A Development Perspective", *World Economy* 27(9):1321–33

Hoeffler, A.E. (2002), "The Augmented Solow Model and the African Growth Debate", *Oxford Bulletin of Economics and Statistics* 64:135–58.

Holmberg, J. (2007), "Natural Resources in Sub-Saharan Africa: Assets and Vulnerabilities". A contribution to the Swedish Government White Paper on Africa, mimeo.

Hulten, C.R. (1996), "Infrastructure Capital and Economic Growth: How well you use it may be more important than how much you have". NBER Working paper no. 5847, Cambridge MA.

Jansen, M. (2006), "Services Trade Liberalization at the Regional level: Does Southern and Eastern Africa Stand to Gain from EPA negotiations?" CEPR Discussion Paper no 5800.

Jayne, T. S., Villarreal, M., Pingali, P., Hemrich, G. (2005), "HIV/AIDS and the Agricultural Sector: Implications for Policy in Eastern and Southern Africa," *The Electronic Journal of Agricultural and Development Economics*, Food and Agriculture Organisation of the United Nations, 2(2):158–81.

Jones, C. (1996), "The Microeconomic Implications of HIV/AIDS". A dissertation submitted to the School of Development Studies of the University of East Anglia in part-fulfilment of the requirements for the degree of Master of Arts.

Kaplinsky, R., Morris, M. (2006), "The Asian Drivers and SSA; MFA Quota Removal and the Portents for African Industrialization?". Institute for Development Studies, University of Sussex and Centre for Research in Innovation Management, University of Brighton.

Kalemli-Ozcan, S. (2006), "AIDS, Reversal of the Demographic Transition and Economic Development: Evidence from Africa". NBER Working Paper 12181, Cambridge, MA.

Klasen, S. (2002), "Low Schooling for Girls, Slower Growth for All? Cross-Country Evidence on the Effect of Gender Inequality in Education on Economic Development", *The World Bank Economic Review* 16(3):345–73.

Klasen, S. (2005), "Economic Growth and Poverty Reduction: Measurement and Policy Issues". Paper prepared for POVNET for the Work Program on Pro Poor Growth, University of Göttingen.

Klasen, S. (2007), "Pro-Poor Growth and Gender Inequality: Insights from new research", *Poverty in Focus,* March 2007, International Poverty Centre, Brasilia.

Knowles, S., Lorgelly, P.K., Dorian Owen, P. (2002), "Are educational gender gaps a brake on economic development? Some cross-country empirical evidence", *Oxford Economic Papers*, 54(1):118–49

Krugman, P. Venables, A.V. (1995). "Globalisation and Inequality of Nations", *Quarterly Journal of Economics* 110:857–80.

Kuznetsov, Y., Abel, C. (2006), "International Migration of Talent, Diaspora Networks, and Development: Overview of Main Issues". In Yevgeny Kuznetsov (ed.), *Diaspora Networks and the International Migration of Skills,* World Bank Institute.

Lewis, D.K, Callaghan, M., Phiri, K., Chipwete, J., Kublin, J.G., Borgstein, E. and Zijlstra, E.E. (2003), "Prevalence and indicators of HIV and AIDS among adults admitted to medical and surgical wards in Blantyre, Malawi", *Transactions of the Royal Society of Tropical Medicine and Hygiene* (2003) 97.

Lorentzen, P., McMillan, J., Wacziarg, R. (2005), "Death and Development". NBER Working Paper 11620, Cambridge, MA.

Martin-Staple, A.(2004), "Proposed 6-year human resource relief programme for the Malawi Health Sector". Report for Duke Centre for International Development, Durham NC.

Mather, D., Donovan, C., Jayne, T.S., Weber, M., Mazhangara, E., Bailey, L., Yoo, K., Yamano, T. and Mghenyi, E (2004), "A Cross-Country Analysis of Household Responses to Adult Mortality in Rural Sub-Saharan Africa: Implications for HIV/AIDS Mitigation and Rural Development Policies". Michigan State University International Development Working Papers 82.

McDonald, S.,Roberts, J. (2006), "AIDS and Economic Growth: A Human Capital Approach", *Journal of Development Economics* 80(1):228–50.

McPherson, M.F. (2003), "Macroeconomic Models of the Impact of HIV/AIDS", Cambridge, Centre for Business and Government, John F. Kennedy School of Government, Harvard University.

Milner, C., Morrissey, O., McKay, A. (2005), "Some Simple Analytics of the Trade and Welfare Effects of Economic Partnership Agreements", *Journal of African Economies* 14(3):327–59.

Ministry of Health (2001), "National Health Account, 2001", Lilongwe.

Mlambo, M.K., Kamara, A.B., Nyende, M. (2007), "Financing Post-Conflict Recovery in Africa: The Role of International Development Assistance". Paper presented at the AERC biannual workshop, Nairobi, mimeo.

Mtika, M. (2003), "Family Transfers in a Subsistence Economy and under a High Incidence of HIV/AIDS: The Case of Rural Malawi", *Journal of Contemporary African Studies* 21(1).

North, D.C. (1990), *Institutions, Institutional Change and Economic Performance.* Cambridge: Cambridge University Press.

O'Connell, S. (2004). "Explaining African Economic Growth: Emerging Lessons from the Growth Project". Paper presented at the biannual AERC workshop, Nairobi.

OECD (2002), "Extracts from the Development Co-operation Review Series on Policy Coherence", http://www.oecd.org/dataoecd/23/16/25497010.pdf

OECD (2003), "Policy coherence: Vital for global development", http://www.oecd.org/depa rtment/0,2688,en_2649_18532957_1_1_1_1_1,00.html

ORC Macro (2007), "Demographic and Health Surveys, various years", available at http:// www.measuredhs.com/

Palmer, D. (2006) "Tackling Malawi's Human Resource Crisis", *Reproductive Health Matters* 14(27).

Pattillo, C., Gupta, S., Carey, K. (2006), "Sustaining Growth Accelerations and Pro-Poor Growth in Africa". IMF Working Paper WP/05/195. Washington DC: IMF.

Pritchett, L., Woolcock, M. (2004), "Solutions when *the* Solution is the Problem: Arraying the Disarray in Development", *World Development* 32(2):191–212.

Rihani, A. (2006), "Keeping the Promise: Five Benefits of Girls' Secondary Education" with L. Kayes and S. Psaki, AED, Center for Gender Equity, Washington.

Rodriguez, F., Rodrik, D. (2000), "Trade Policy and Economic Growth: A Sceptics Guide to the Cross-national Evidence". Mimeo, University of Maryland and Harvard University.

Rosen, S., Simon, J., Thea, D. M. and Vincent, J. R. (2000), "Care and Treatment to Extend the Working Lives of HIV-Positive Employees: Calculating the Benefits to Business", *South African Journal of Science* No. 96, June, pp. 300–305.

Sachs, J. , McArthur, J.W., Schmidt-Traub, G., Kruk, M., Bahadur, C., Faye, M., McCord, G. (2004), "Ending Africa' s Poverty Trap", *Brookings Papers on Economic Activity* No 1:117–240.

Salinas, G., Haacker, M. (2006), "HIV/AIDS: The Impact on Poverty and Inequality". IMF Working Paper No. 06/126

Shah, M. K., Osborne, N., Mbilizi, T. and Vilili, G. (2002), "Impact of HIV/AIDS on Agricultural Productivity and Rural Livelihoods in the Central Region of Malawi", CARE International Malawi

Stosky, J.G. (2006), "Gender and Its Relevance to Macroeconomic Policy: A Survey". IMF Working Paper WP/06/233.

Subramanian, U. Matthijs, M. (2007). "Can Sub-Saharan Africa Leap into Global Network Trade?" World Bank Policy Research Working Paper 4112.

Sweden (2001), Globkom, the Committee on Sweden's policy for global development SOU 2001:96.

Tarp, F. (2006), "Aid and Development", *Swedish Economic Policy Review* 16(2).

Taylor, A.M. (2002), "Globalization, Trade and Development: Some Lessons from History". NBER Working Paper 9326, Cambridge MA.

Tsangarides, C.G. (2005), "Growth Empirics under Model Uncertainty: Is Africa Different?" IMF Working Paper 05/18.

Zafar, Ali (2007), The Growing Relationship Between China and Sub-Saharan Africa: Macro-economic, Trade Investment and Aid Links", *The World Bank Observer* 22(1):103–30.

UCDP/PRIO (2007), "Armed Conflict Dataset 1946–2005". (http://www.prio.no/cwp/armedconflict/current/Conflict_List_1946-2005.pdf)

UN (2005), *Investing in Development: A Practical Plan to Achieve the Millennium Development Goals.* New York.

UNAIDS (2006), "2006 Report on the global AIDS epidemic", United Nations and Joint United Nations Programme on HIV/AIDS (UNAIDS), Geneva, Switzerland.

UN Comtrade, Database, internet.

UNDP (2005), H*uman Development Report 2005:International cooperation at a crossroads:Aid, trade and security in an unequal world.* New York: UNDP.

UN Population Division (2004), "The Impact of AIDS". New York: United Nations.

Werker, Eric. Amrita Ahuja, and Brian Wendell (2006), "Male Circumcison and the Economic Impact of AIDS in Africa". Mimeo, Harvard Business School.

Whiteside, A., O'Grady, M. (2002), "AIDS and the Private Sector: Lessons from Southern Africa". Chapter 6 in *Sida Studies* no. 7. One Step Further – Responses to HIV/AIDS, Stockholm, pp.116–37.

World Bank (2004), "Cost, financing and school effectiveness of education in Malawi: A future of limited choices and endless opportunities", Country Status Report, African Region Human Development Working Paper Series, Washington DC.

World Bank (2005), *Global Monitoring Report* 2005, Washington DC.

World Bank (2006), *Global Monitoring Report* 2006, Washington DC.

World Bank (2007a), *World Development Indicators,* Online 2007.

World Bank (2007b), *Global Development Finance*, Online 2007.

World Health Organisation (2005a), "World Health Report 2005: make every mother and child count", Geneva.

World Health Organisation (2005b), "Global Atlas of the Health Workforce", available on-line: http://www.who.int/globalatlas/default.asp [2005-08-31].

Young, A. (2005a), "The Gift of Dying: The Tragedy of AIDS and the Welfare of Future African Generations", *Quarterly Journal of Economics* 120(2).

Young, A. (2005b), "Tin Sorrow to Bring Forth Children: Fertility amidst the Plague of HIV". Mimeo, University of Chicago.

CURRENT AFRICAN ISSUES PUBLISHED BY THE INSTITUTE
Recent issues in the series are available electronically
for download free of charge www.nai.uu.se

1. *South Africa, the West and the Frontline States. Report from a Seminar.* 1981, 34 pp, (out-of print)

2. Maja Naur, *Social and Organisational Change in Libya.* 1982, 33 pp, (out-of print)

3. *Peasants and Agricultural Production in Africa. A Nordic Research Seminar. Follow-up Reports and Discussions.* 1981, 34 pp, (out-of print)

4. Ray Bush & S. Kibble, *Destabilisation in Southern Africa, an Overview.* 1985, 48 pp, (out-of print)

5. Bertil Egerö, *Mozambique and the Southern African Struggle for Liberation.* 1985, 29 pp, (out-of print)

6. Carol B.Thompson, *Regional Economic Polic under Crisis Condition. Southern African Development.* 1986, 34 pp, (out-of print)

7. Inge Tvedten, *The War in Angola, Internal Conditions for Peace and Recovery.* 1989, 14 pp, (out-of print)

8. Patrick Wilmot, *Nigeria's Southern Africa Policy 1960–1988.* 1989, 15 pp, (out-of print)

9. Jonathan Baker, *Perestroika for Ethiopia: In Search of the End of the Rainbow?* 1990, 21 pp, (out-of print)

10. Horace Campbell, *The Siege of Cuito Cuanavale.* 1990, 35 pp, (out-of print)

11. Maria Bongartz, *The Civil War in Somalia. Its genesis and dynamics.* 1991, 26 pp, (out-of print)

12. Shadrack B.O. Gutto, *Human and People's Rights in Africa. Myths, Realities and Prospects.* 1991, 26 pp, (out-of print)

13. Said Chikhi, Algeria. *From Mass Rebellion to Workers' Protest.* 1991, 23 pp, (out-of print)

14. Bertil Odén, *Namibia's Economic Links to South Africa.* 1991, 43 pp, (out-of print)

15. Cervenka Zdenek, *African National Congress Meets Eastern Europe. A Dialogue on Common Experiences.* 1992, 49 pp, ISBN 91-7106-337-4, (out-of print)

16. Diallo Garba, *Mauritania–The Other Apartheid?* 1993, 75 pp, ISBN 91-7106-339-0, (out-of print)

17. Zdenek Cervenka and Colin Legum, *Can National Dialogue Break the Power of Terror in Burundi?* 1994, 30 pp, ISBN 91-7106-353-6, (out-of print)

18. Erik Nordberg and Uno Winblad, *Urban Environmental Health and Hygiene in Sub-Saharan Africa.* 1994, 26 pp, ISBN 91-7106-364-1, (out-of print)

19. Chris Dunton and Mai Palmberg, *Human Rights and Homosexuality in Southern Africa.* 1996, 48 pp, ISBN 91-7106-402-8, (out-of print)

20. Georges Nzongola-Ntalaja *From Zaire to the Democratic Republic of the Congo.* 1998, 18 pp, ISBN 91-7106-424-9, (out-of print)

21. Filip Reyntjens, *Talking or Fighting? Political Evolution in Rwanda and Burundi, 1998–1999.* 1999, 27 pp, ISBN 91-7106-454-0, SEK 80.-

22. Herbert Weiss, *War and Peace in the Democratic Republic of the Congo.* 1999, 28 pp, ISBN 91-7106-458-3, SEK 80,-

23. Filip Reyntjens, *Small States in an Unstable Region – Rwanda and Burundi, 1999–2000,* 2000, 24 pp, ISBN 91-7106-463-X, (out-of print)

24. Filip Reyntjens, *Again at the Crossroads: Rwanda and Burundi, 2000–2001.* 2001, 25 pp, ISBN 91-7106-483-4, (out-of print)

25. Henning Melber, *The New African Initiative and the African Union. A Preliminary Assessment and Documentation.* 2001, 36 pp, ISBN 91-7106-486-9, (out-of print)

26. Dahilon Yassin Mohamoda, *Nile Basin Cooperation. A Review of the Literature.* 2003, 39 pp, ISBN 91-7106-512-1, SEK 90,-

27. Henning Melber (ed.), *Media, Public Discourse and Political Contestation in Zimbabwe.* 2004, 39 pp, ISBN 91-7106-534-2, SEK 90,-

28. Georges Nzongola-Ntalaja, *From Zaire to the Democratic Republic of the Congo.* Second and Revised Edition. 2004, 23 pp, ISBN-91-7106-538-5, (out-of print)

29. Henning Melber (ed.), *Trade, Development, Cooperation – What Future for Africa?* 2005, 44 pp, ISBN 91-7106-544-X, SEK 90,-

30. Kaniye S.A. Ebeku, *The Succession of Faure Gnassingbe to the Togolese Presidency – An International Law Perspective.* 2005, 32 pp, ISBN 91-7106-554-7, SEK 90,-

31. Jeffrey V. Lazarus, Catrine Christiansen, Lise Rosendal Østergaard, Lisa Ann Richey, *Models for Life – Advancing antiretroviral therapy in sub-Saharan Africa.* 2005, 33 pp, ISBN 91-7106-556-3, SEK 90,-

32. Charles Manga Fombad and Zein Kebonang, *AU, NEPAD and the APRM – Democratisation Efforts Explored.* Edited by Henning Melber. 2006, 56 pp, ISBN 91-7106-569-5, SEK 90,-

33. Pedro Pinto Leite, Claes Olsson, Magnus Schöldtz, Toby Shelley, Pål Wrange, Hans Corell and Karin Scheele, *The Western Sahara Conflict – The Role of Natural Resources in Decolonization.* Edited by Claes Olsson. 2006, 32 pp, ISBN 91-7106-571-7, SEK 90,-

34. Jassey, Katja and Stella Nyanzi, *How to Be a "Proper" Woman in the Times of HIV and AIDS.* 2007, 35 pp, ISBN 91-7106-574-1, SEK 90,-

35. Lee, Margaret, Henning Melber, Sanusha Naidu and Ian Taylor, *China in Africa.* Compiled by Henning Melber. 2007, 47 pp, ISBN 978-91-7106-589-6, SEK 90,-

36. Nathaniel King, *Conflict as Integration. Youth Aspiration to Personhood in the Teleology of Sierra Leone's 'Senseless War'.* 2007, 32 pp, ISBN 978-91-7106-604-6, SEK 90,-

37. Aderanti Adepoju, *Migration in sub-Saharan Africa.* 2008. 70 pp, ISBN 978-91-7106-620-6 SEK 90,-

38. Bo Malmberg, *Demography and the development potential of sub-Saharan Africa.* 2008, 39 pp, 978-91-7106-621-3, SEK 90,-

39. Johan Holmberg, *Natural resources in sub-Saharan Africa: Assets and vulnerabilities.* 2008, 52 pp, 978-91-7106-624-4, SEK 90,-

40. Arne Bigsten and Dick Durevall, *The African economy and its role in the world economy.* 2008, 66 pp, 978-91-7106-625-1, SEK 90,-

www.ingramcontent.com/pod-product-compliance
Lightning Source LLC
Chambersburg PA
CBHW080056280326
41934CB00014B/3329